Managing Your Time With The Help Of Microsoft® Outlook

by

Penny Mayhew

COPYRIGHT

CANVIN PUBLISHING

ISBN- 978-0-9930820-54

First published in December 2016
Canvin Publishing
Milton Keynes, UK

Printed and Bound in Great Britain

Contents

INTRODUCTION

This book is for anyone that wants to learn how to manage their time better. I stress the word *'manage'* - a common misconception of Time Management is that we can increase the time we have each day. But that's impossible - no matter what we do, there will only ever be 24 hours in the day maximum, and nothing can change that fact. So, we need to manage our time better and more efficiently if we want to keep on top of everything.

Our days are becoming busier, the demands upon us more intense than ever before, and it's easy to become overwhelmed and, quite often, exhausted and stressed. So, this book is designed to help you explore useful strategies and techniques you can use to take back some control.

I guess you're here either because you want to change something about how you manage your time, or because you're interested in the different strategies out there to help fit all the things you need to do into your day. Maybe you're fed up with time thieves stealing your precious minutes for their own use. Perhaps you're wondering where your time seems to go every day.

But this book is not just about Time Management. There's the added bonus of getting into the nitty gritty of Microsoft® Outlook in terms of how it can help you manage your time. Yes, Microsoft® Outlook isn't just there for sending and receiving emails. There's a whole host of hidden gems just waiting to be discovered which can really help you with the strategies covered in the first part of this book. The Time Management theory, and the tools available in Microsoft® Outlook, work brilliantly together.

Don't worry if you don't know too much about Microsoft® Outlook, we'll have a really good look at the key features throughout the book. And it doesn't really matter if you have an older version of the software as you can do most things we cover in other versions too. The screen captures you see throughout the book are taken from the Windows version of Microsoft® Outlook 2016, as are the instructions, and so you may need to search around your computer screen for the icons and tools if you're using a different version. You may even be able to use some of the features in other non-Microsoft® software you use for emailing and managing your calendar and appointments.

Now, if you're struggling to juggle your time and tasks at the moment, it's understandable that you might be worried about having to take time out of your busy schedule to read this book in the first place. Let me reassure you - it's a worthwhile investment taking some time out to help YOU! We spend so much time rushing around to fit everything in, and to donate our time and energy to others and their needs, so sometimes we need to stand back and examine where our time currently goes and how to utilise those precious minutes each day more efficiently. You're worth it!

Before we start, I'll share with you the reason I've written this book. Time Management didn't come naturally to me but I was lucky to have worked in some really interesting jobs over the years which taught me a common skill — how to prioritise a list of tasks. For example, I worked in a busy Emergency Services Control room quite early in my career and it was quite a shock to the system having to learn quickly how to prioritise - which jobs required immediate attendance, who was the most appropriate and qualified resource to allocate etc. and I had to learn rapidly as a mistake could have serious repercussions and consequences. Prioritisation has featured in many of my jobs since then. I've been a Training Consultant for 20 years, regularly working with companies, groups and individuals as a Time Management facilitator, coach and IT trainer. And what I love most about my job is seeing a positive change for people, with an increase in their productivity, efficiency and, just as important (if not more so), a work/life balance.

So, although I can't give you more than 24 hours in a day (It's non-negotiable, I'm afraid) my aim for this book is that it helps you to make the most of each and every minute you have, and to consider using a tool to help - Microsoft® Outlook.

(If you prefer learning by watching and listening, check out www.pennymayhew.com for details of online courses!)

Time Management Theory

When Are You Most Efficient?

Effective time management requires a commitment to change and you need to accept that right now at the very start of the book. There's the famous quote, credited to the automotive tycoon Henry Ford:

"If you always do what you've always done, you'll always get what you've always got..."

Actually, the official source of the citation is still disputed. It's been credited to several people and in slight variants, such as 'If you continue to think like you've always thought, you'll continue to get what you've always got.' Whoever actually said it, it's a powerful message – if you are not willing to change how you manage your time, don't expect your Time Management to improve. It will just stay the same.

Like many things in life, the success of Time Management comes down to planning. So, think about your last year. If you work, imagine yourself in your job, carrying out your daily tasks, working through your schedule to make sure everything gets done. Or, imagine yourself at home, with your weekly and daily chores and responsibilities, all needing to be completed before they get out of hand or are forgotten. In the last year, try to think about the day you felt at your most efficient, where you completed everything that was needed, with nothing left outstanding. All your emails were answered, your washing cleaned and ironed, the house spotless, the paperwork sorted and filed away. Can you think what day it was?

It was the day before you went on holiday! Whether a one or two-week vacation/staycation, or a few days away, you'd have prepared yourself and cleared all, or most, of the jobs on your To Do list before packing up and turning off the lights. It's what we do when we know we have only a small timeframe to get things done to the standard required.

At work, we clear our emails, put plans in place for while we're away, delegate if possible and clear our desks of anything of low priority. And, at home, we wash and iron to pack our clothes, clean the house to make sure it's fit for when we return, pay any bills that might be due whilst we're away – we may even mow the lawn so it doesn't look like a jungle when we get back.

We seem to fit in so much more than we do in a normal day. But how? Well, we prioritise the most important tasks, probably make a list and then work through as smartly and efficiently as we can. If anyone interrupts, or tries to steal our time, we're at our most assertive. We have no problem saying 'Actually, I can't do that right now as I must get this task done before I go away. I'll look into that when I get back.' We don't feel guilty or rude because we know our jobs have to be done before we can leave. If we could be like this every other day of the year, our Time Management would be sorted.

Every day we are faced with a multitude of tasks and things to do, and we juggle them as best we can to make sure we are as productive as possible. But do you know exactly how you currently spend your time? What tasks do you prioritise? How long do you spend doing each of your jobs? If you had to list exactly what you did this day last week, could you? The chances are you wouldn't be able to. Once the day has gone, we move on to the next and start all over again. We are often too busy or pre-occupied to remember exactly what was important to us this time last week, and even less likely if the tasks were low priority, mundane and routine matters.

Before we can start to work on our Time Management skills we need to examine the way we spend our time. One way to do this is to keep a time log for a few days.

Once you start listing what you do, what time of day you do it and how long you spend on a task, you might be surprised. For example, you may spot that quite a huge chunk of your time was snatched by others; those colleagues that somehow managed to pass a job onto you without you noticing until it was too late, or a friend dropping in to see you at home and staying for hours because their own 'To Do' list was empty.

Date				
What	Start Time	End Time	How Long?	Comments

Here's an example of a Time Log. You can create one using Microsoft® Word, Microsoft® Excel or other similar software, but there's a free template to download (go to the Resources section at the back of the book to find out how) plus an example of a completed log.

We'll be referring back to it later in the book and so make sure you complete it as best as possible. The more you put in, the more you'll learn! Make sure you include everything, even if you feel it is something that just has to be done and that you can't change, or one that's non-negotiable. You may prefer to design your own using either pen and paper - it doesn't matter what it looks like, it just matters that you do it! If we are going to change how we use our time, we need to examine where it all goes.

When you've completed the time log move onto the next chapter. You might not like what you find when you examine that log, but remember your commitment to change...

Examining Your Habitual Choices

So, if you completed the time log from the previous chapter you should now have a breakdown of everything you've been doing over the last few days, and how long you spent doing them. I agree it's a bit of a chore completing the log, and takes up quite a lot of your valuable and precious minutes throughout the day, but it's very important to analyse the current use of your time so that you can make changes. In particular, it will give you an insight into the importance of planning efficiently. You'll see what tasks are urgent and important and which were things you hadn't set out to do but were 'given' or 'donated to' by others.

Take a look at your task log and think about the following:

- Which of the tasks were planned?
- Which of the items on the list were things you were asked to do by someone else?
- Do you feel any of the tasks were unnecessary but a habit?
- Could you have delegated any of the tasks to someone else. For example, a work task to a colleague, or a home chore to another member of the household?
- How many of the tasks did you complete from start to end without being disturbed?
- How many of the tasks did you start and stop several times because of other demands or interruptions?
- Which of the tasks do you wish you could have scrapped, and would never have to do again?

An important point to remember is:

"just because you've always done something, it doesn't mean you always have to..."

You may find that some of those tasks are not absolutely necessary and add no value at all. You do them because either a) you always have or b) others expect you to.

Another important consideration is how you felt when you were carrying out the tasks on your list. Did it make you feel:
- Happy
- Annoyed and reluctant
- Tired or exhausted
- Low in mood

We can't always stop doing tasks just because they have a negative effect on us as some of them are essential and necessary. But maybe we could look at moving those tasks to a more convenient or appropriate part of the day. Personally I try to do the jobs I dislike most at the start of the day, so that they're done and finished, and I won't have to think about them anymore. My mood instantly lifts and I can get on with my day with a much happier and energetic frame of mind. If I leave them till later I'd spend the day dreading it. The tasks that make me really happy, I try to leave until last, so I end on a high. But, maybe it would work out better the other way around for you - we're all different.

Whether your task log is on paper or in electronic format, highlight any tasks which have raised questions in your mind. Think about how and why you did them. What would the repercussions have been had you not completed the job at all? Who could you have delegated the task to? And, be honest with yourself over this one – did you complete any of those tasks because it was the expectation of someone else that you do so? Maybe it's time to challenge the tendency to say yes, which we will cover in another chapter.

Look at your list and make a note next to each task about how you felt when you were doing it. Use the smiley face system if that works for you, or, make a grading system of 1-5, 1 being thoroughly miserable to 5 being great! For the moment, keep hold of this task log as we'll continue to refer to it as we go through the rest of the book.

The Pareto Principle

Have you heard of the Pareto Principle?

In 1906 an economist, Vilfredo Pareto, created a formula to describe the unequal distribution of wealth in his country of Italy. He found that just 20% of the people owned 80% of the land. This became known as the Pareto Principle and, over time, has evolved to become a formula applied to many different situations. One example is that 80% of results come from 20% effort.

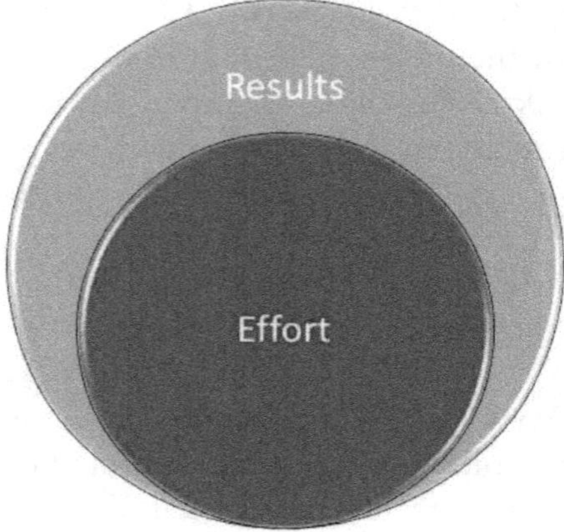

It's obviously better to have it this way around. Imagine how your own life would be if you spent 80% of your time (effort), working hard and at all hours, yet only achieve 20% in terms of results and progression.

To apply the Pareto Principle to your Time Management you need to work out which 20% of your own tasks produce 80% of the results, whether in business or at home. Then, you can spend more time and energy on those jobs. Let's say that we work out 20% of the tasks we do are vital, and 80% are trivial. The 20% is what really matters as it will produce 80% of the results we strive for. If we find ourselves running out of time in our day, then we can concentrate on that 20% of important and urgent tasks and still achieve a high ratio in terms of results.

But what are the most vital tasks in your list of things to do? We'll take a good look at this in the next chapter but, for the moment, they are the tasks that are most productive, the ones that give you the best results and move you forward in your day, week and life in general.

This sounds straight forward but it's not quite that simple... turning down jobs we need to complete will mean doing things a little differently and maybe out of your comfort zone. You might have to start saying no to people that request things from you, sometimes loved ones, people that are important to you. Or maybe you'll need to make yourself unavailable so you don't get disturbed, and this can leave you feeling guilty and selfish. You're going to need to challenge every job and task in terms of establishing if it's a waste of time and effort, or if it's really necessary.

All of this may feel awkward and uncomfortable to start with, but remember how I introduced you to the book by saying how we need to commit to change if we want to see results.

- Just try the 80/20 principle for a few days to see what happens. You might be concentrating on the wrong tasks if:
- You're working on jobs that other people want you to invest your time and energy in, but it means you get nothing in return. Instead, you should be feeling that the task is advancing you in some way, whether in business or your personal life.
- You're working on things that aren't making the best use of your skills and expertise.
- You take a long time to get things done, either because you do not have the skills for the task, or you're not sure as to why you're doing it. You'll know it's working when you feel good carrying out the job or chore, even if it's something that's not comfortable or straightforward to do, but because you can see the purpose.

Ultimately, you need to feel happy and unstressed! Being aware of what's vital, and what isn't, is a major step in managing your time more effectively.

In the next chapter we will look at how to decide if a task is urgent and important, and whether this means it is vital or not. It might surprise you to find that those tasks we think are urgent are actually someone else's priority and not our own, and could be delegated or removed from our list of things to do.

Using a Time Matrix

The Pareto Principle highlights the need to evaluate which of our tasks are vital so that you can spend your energy and time on those tasks to produce the most effective results. But, how can we decide which tasks are the most important? This chapter looks at how we can analyse our activities, to see which are urgent and/or important, and it's called the Time Management Matrix.

Some of the jobs you do may be urgent *and* important. For example, emergencies, vital meetings, medical appointments and technological failures.

But, not all tasks fit *both* of these categories. For example, you may have a task that involves planning and designing. It could be urgent, as you've a deadline, but it might not necessarily be important. Or vice versa.

And some tasks fit neither of these categories, but still need to be done, such as reading documentation and emails of a non-urgent nature.

To decide which tasks are vital in line with the Pareto Principle, try using the Time Management Matrix:

	Urgent	Not Urgent
Important	**Do Now**	**Plan To Do**
Not Important	**Reject and Explain**	**Resist and Cease**

Let's look at the **Important** tasks first. We can see in the Matrix that Important tasks can be Urgent or Not-Urgent. An **urgent important** task needs to be done right now, such as an emergency or a problem resolution. Examples of Important AND Urgent tasks are:

- Demands from Supervisors or Customers
- Planned tasks and project work now due
- Meetings and appointments
- Reports and other submissions
- Staff issues or needs
- Problem resolution, firefighting, fixes

These tasks need to be prioritised according to how urgent they actually are. But be careful if you're spending the majority of your time on tasks like these - because they have to be done right now, they can leave you feeling stressed and exhausted as the tasks consume you and take over your life...

Important tasks which are **not urgent** include things such as research, form filling, system development and scheduling. They are critical to success but are things you can plan to do rather than jump into immediately.

We also have the tasks which are **not important**, but that could still be **urgent**. A not-important, urgent task could be a trivial request from someone else, or an apparent emergency. You'll need to scrutinise the task and really analyse the demand. Be prepared to reject it and explain to people involved why, in a sensitive manner. This is when it can be tough, but it's the only way.

Lastly we have the **not important**, and **not-urgent**, tasks. These are jobs such as surfing the internet and cigarette breaks, chat and gossip, and the reading of non-urgent materials which are irrelevant in the context of other 'stuff' going on around you. They can eat into our precious time and should be minimised or stopped altogether.

Look at your task list and think about where they fit within the time matrix. Which box would contain the majority of your tasks? And, are you putting your time and energy into the right things?

We'll explore this further in the chapter called 'Learning to Prioritise', to enable you to have a better understanding of how you spend your time, and how efficient your time management is.

What's Holding You Back?

Catching The Time Thieves

So, you might be a great planner and have all your tasks worked out and set for the day ahead, whether it be for work or at home. And everything goes perfectly until... a time thief comes along.

Time thieves can be people, such as your colleague who pops up to ask you to collate some information urgently, or a visitor at your door when you're in the middle of something important. A time thief can equally be a task that is put on you, such as some urgent paperwork to complete, or a phone call that comes in and wipes out 30 minutes of your precious time that you'd planned to use doing something else.

Here's some of our common time thieves:

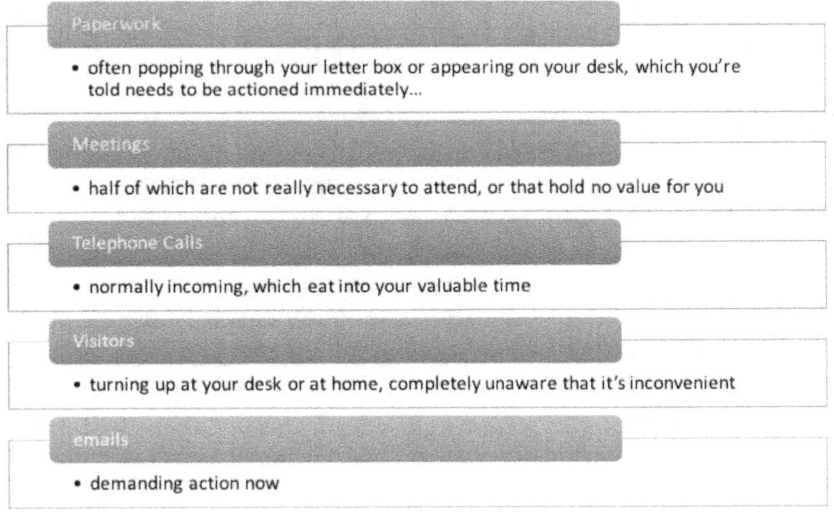

Have a look at your Task Log and see if any of the tasks were the work of 'time thieves'. Even if they're not, there's bound to have been at least one occasion where a time thief came along and stopped you carrying out another task on your list, or made it take you ten times longer than it should have done.

It's time to get to grips with those time thieves. We need to eliminate, or at least reduce, the impact they have on our daily planning, our energy and our life/work balance.

Let's see how we can stop them in their tracks by examining each of the common time thieves in a bit more detail.

Paperwork

One of the top culprits is paperwork - it's often absolutely necessary to complete but can take up a huge amount of your time. So, before becoming buried under mounds of paperwork and documents, first think about if it's only you that can complete the task. How about delegating it to someone else at work, or in the home? It's not always easy to give it to someone else, as we often feel we can do it more quickly by ourselves, and to our *standard*. But if it's becoming a burden, and taking up your precious time, you have got to start letting go. Could it be broken down into chunks, so you do a little here and there, rather than in one large stint?

Meetings

I think we all have experience of attending meetings that have felt pointless at times, or unnecessary. You may have asked, 'Why am I even here? This is nothing to do with me!' We can't always choose not to go, as our attendance is sometimes mandatory, but we can try to help meetings be as streamlined and effective as possible. Is it essential that you attend, or could someone go in your place and feed the information back? Do you need to attend the full meeting, or just part of it? Is there an agenda? If there's no agenda, ask for one, as this is an opportunity to make suggestions about the content and to question if the meeting could be divided up into subjects so that not all of the attendees need to be there at the same time. And, is the meeting at a convenient time or could it to be moved so as to free up more of your schedule for other tasks? Sometimes meetings happen on a particular day, and at a particular time, just because it always has... challenge it if this is the case.

Telephone calls

Most of us don't have the freedom to unplug the telephone or refuse to take incoming calls. But sometimes we receive calls that are unnecessary or better dealt with by someone else. If receiving calls at home, Caller ID is useful as you can see who is calling first and choose to answer or not. It's not being rude; it's just taking control of your own time. At work, even though Caller ID may be activated on your phone, your company policy may be to answer the phone immediately it rings, no matter what. But, you still have some control. Tell the caller it's not a convenient time to talk right now, but that you'll ring them back later, and give them a time (and keep to it!) If someone else can deal with the matter, transfer the call. And be firm with the caller. Let people know you haven't got much time to speak and to get to the point as quickly as possible. Don't feel it's being difficult, they're stealing your time and energy!

Visitors

It's not a problem when people turn up to see you at a prearranged date and time as you've planned this into your schedule or diary, whether at home or work. It's the unexpected visitors that cause us a problem, and it's not easy to refuse their visit when they arrive as it feels a little rude and anti-social. But, a visitor at your front door when you're right in the middle of an important chore is a huge drain on your time. If you don't feel able to refuse their visit, maybe say that they're welcome in but you only have half hour for a quick coffee and chat as you've something important to do. Or, if it's at work and they turn up at your desk, tell them you're in the middle of something but will pop and see them later. If you've the luxury of an office door, keep it closed when you're up to your eyes in work!

Emails

As for emails, we've several chapters in this book about how to help deal with those time thieves!

A most demanding and aggressive time thief of all is... procrastination! Yes, we're often responsible for our own poor time management. We put off the jobs we don't want to do, in favour of the nice, pleasant and quick ones, and then the big task gets left until tomorrow, then the next day, then the next day. We'll look at this in the next chapter.

Procrastination

So, we've looked at some of the time thieves and can see how we can take more back. But what about procrastination? Are you guilty of putting things off? Do you suddenly find something much more interesting to do, even though it's not as much of a priority as the task you're supposed to be working on? We all do it, to some extent. But it's a drain on our time and energy. Procrastination causes a whole range of emotions, including frustration and guilt. Plus, it ultimately means that certain jobs won't get done. It's time to get it sorted!

The bottom line is, essential tasks need to be done and they need to be done now. Don't put them off, it won't work and will only make things worse. Look through your Task Log you created and, in particular, the essential tasks in the list. Did you do these first? Or did you leave any until later in the day? Were some of the tasks even carried over to the next day? If so, what did this feel like? And, why did you procrastinate?

Well, it's something we all do from time to time. We're not talking about shifting tasks due to prioritisation, because something more urgent came along out of the blue. We're talking about a purposeful decision to not do something that we know must be done right now. Often we do it because the task is boring or unpleasant. For example, at work this could be filing, at home it could be tidying a huge pile of paperwork that's been building up for months.

Other times it could be because we're nervous or apprehensive about what's required of us. Maybe we don't think we're qualified or good enough to do the task, or that we'll look silly or unprofessional if we get it wrong and fail. We let our lack of confidence get in the way.

If we become a serial procrastinator we almost begin to believe that the tasks will magically disappear, particularly if we leave it long enough. Maybe others will forget they're waiting on something from us. Or, if we're really lucky, someone else will do it for us. But, the opposite actually happens. The task grows in size along with our stress levels. Then, our energy levels deplete with the frustration and feelings of failure and ineffectiveness. We begin to have to hide from those that are waiting, and choose to avoid phone calls, emails and visits, whilst the task sits there staring at us.

So, how can we beat procrastination? Here's some tips:

- Make a To Do list and ensure you put deadlines against each task (we'll cover this in more detail during the Task section).
- Try breaking your task down into smaller pieces. Quite often, the tasks we put off are huge, making them seem almost impossible. If you chip away, a little at a time, it's much more do-able and you'll be motivated by the progress you make.
- Can you delegate the task, or at least a part of it, to someone else? If you can't, consider having someone support you, by encouraging you and helping to set realistic deadlines.
- Really think about your day and try to work out when you're at your most effective. Are your energy levels at their highest in the morning? Then, get those tasks you've been dreading out of the way first thing. The rest of the day will be plain sailing! Do you have an energy slump in the afternoon? If so, tasks such as reading documentation and concentrating on facts and figures can be almost impossible, so choose to do them at a different time, and use the afternoon to carry out tasks that require you to move around and communicate. This will help to banish the yawns!

Learning to Say No

So, you're sat at your desk with your 'To Do' list in front of you, working through your tasks happily, satisfied that you're totally on track to get everything done. You've beat procrastination and thrown yourself straight in. Then, you're suddenly aware of someone hovering nearby... you try to ignore them but, in the end, you feel rude and uncomfortable and so you look up and they rush towards you with a job they want you to do. And they want it done right now. You know that this means your own tasks won't be completed as planned and that you'll have jobs left to carry over to the next day which is already busy and full of things to do. Yet, it's likely you'll say yes to the time thief intruder...

Often we say 'yes, sure, I can do that for you'. But, when we do this, their task becomes ours and takes the lead in the priority stakes. As we start to realise the effect it will have on us, they're smiling - they know that their task is now progressing and they can forget about it, freeing up time for their other jobs.

And this happens at home too, such as when someone turns up at the door unannounced, hoping for a chat and a coffee, when all you want to do is get your paperwork sorted, or the packing done before you go away on holiday.

So why do we find it so hard to say no, and what can we do about it?

We find it hard because we don't want to disappoint people, let them down, or appear rude. It's nicer and easier to say yes and, at the end of the day, we all want to be liked and to not cause ill feeling. But, setting boundaries is one of the most important skills, both personally and professionally, that we can master. We need to be able to say no to things which will cause us problems, that will not allow us to progress and also which we will not enjoy. Remember that if you say no to something you do not want to do, you are saying yes to the things that are vital, important and a necessary task for YOU.

Here's a tip for when someone turns up at your desk with a job they need you to do right now. If you don't feel comfortable saying no immediately, tell them you will look at it when you've finished your current task and will get back to them with a time that you will have it completed. This sets out expectations and boundaries and also gives you breathing space. Plus, it doesn't feel as awkward or rude as you're not saying a definite no, you're just saying it will be when you're able.

Are you a member of a group or board that you no longer want to be part of but are finding it impossible to leave? If you're not a) enjoying it b) finding any benefits from attending or c) feel it's a waste of time that could be spent elsewhere, then LEAVE! Resign from the board, remove yourself from the group, and move on. There's more important things you could be spending your time doing.

And what about meetings? Are you really needed or are you just expected to always attend? If there's no need for you to be there then decline the invite. If you've been invited through an email in Microsoft® Outlook, it's fairly easy to do, you just click the Decline button.

Setting boundaries and sticking to them is an essential life skill and, once you've got on top of it, you may need to educate those around you. Don't feel bad about saying, 'Actually, I can't do this right now. I'll look at it tomorrow morning.'

Your time belongs to you and is precious. Protect it!

Learning to Prioritise

In an earlier chapter we looked at the Time Matrix, to work out which of our tasks are urgent, important, non-urgent and non-important. We also looked at the Pareto Principle, where 20% of our tasks are vital and produce 80% of results.

But how easy is it to prioritise our tasks to make sure we focus on the right ones? We can be easily over-whelmed by the amount of work we have to do, especially when the deadlines are all fairly close together.

The essential tool here is a To Do list. This is a list of all your tasks but prioritised in order of urgency and importance. If you have a list, you can make sure that everything is in one place and there's no risk of forgetting something important. And the actual prioritisation element allows you to deal with the things that need immediate action, and protects you from being over-loaded with work.

So, how do we make the list and decide how to order it in terms of priority?

Well, first write down everything that needs to be done. For the moment, this can be on paper, but later we'll look at how we can use Microsoft® Outlook to make an electronic version. When writing down the jobs to do you may find yourself creating a huge task that is going to take hours, so break it down into bite sized chunks. This will make it much more realistic in terms of a timely achievement. You may want to keep two lists, one for personal matters and one for work. Combining the two can make things extra complicated and just adds to the difficulties of maintaining a life/work balance.

Once your list is made it's time to go through it and prioritise. Use the Time Matrix to mark those that are urgent and important (the vital tasks). If you have quite a few, prioritise them in terms of deadlines. If they have similar deadlines, prioritise those tasks in terms of productivity and progression. Remember the Pareto

Principle – which of them will be vital to achieve that 80% of results?

Then, work through your list and tick tasks to show when they're completed. The actual physical act of ticking is rewarding and satisfying, and helps to motivate you to continue working through your jobs. At the end of the day review the list - the tasks not yet completed can be moved onto tomorrow's list and re-prioritised.

When we get to the chapter about Tasks in Microsoft® Outlook you'll see the benefits of having an electronic list compared to paper. If it is a paper based list, you may need to recreate it each day, as some of the tasks are carried over and need to fit in with the new order of prioritisation. If in electronic format, this is easily done. Tasks can be re-ordered, marked as complete and even assigned to other people in just a few clicks. And, remember too that you can sync your list with other devices, such as your smart phone or tablet.

Learning to Delegate

When you've sifted through your list of tasks, eliminated the time thieves and prioritised those jobs that are most vital, what do you do if there are still not enough hours in your day to get everything completed? After all, it doesn't matter how organised you are, or how hard you work, you will still only have a maximum of 24 hours in a day. Some of those hours must be spent resting, eating and relaxing to make sure there's balance in your life to keep healthy and happy. So, you'll only have a set number of hours left to work with your tasks.

It's a known fact that if you're really good at your job, and doing everything you need to do, others will expect even more from you and the pressure this creates can become unbearable. You suddenly find new jobs being thrown at you and added to your list, whether this is at work or home.

So, something to consider is to ask for help. Yes, I can almost feel you flinching... very few of us embrace the concept of asking for help. But why?

Well, maybe we feel it's a weakness and gives the impression we're not in control, or able to cope. It can also be difficult to let a job go, particularly when you've spent a lot of time researching, planning and investing your energy. So, to hand it over to someone else at the final hurdle can feel hugely disappointing. Then, there's our own expectations of the standard to which a job should be done. Who's guilty of saying, 'they won't take as much care as I do,' or, 'they won't do as much of a thorough job'? I definitely have had those thoughts...

But, delegation enables you to use your time and skills better and is also a great opportunity to let others build on their own skills whilst being coached by you along the way. For example, a more inexperienced member of the team would have a safe environment to learn a new skill in the workplace. Or, at home, your child would have the opportunity to learn a new life skill that they'll need in the future, such as having a go at cooking the evening meal whilst you sort out important paperwork. Delegation offers benefits on both sides.

Take a look at your Task Log and see if you feel any of those jobs could have been delegated to someone else. Question any barriers you might instantly put up, and ask yourself these questions:

- Is there someone else available that you think would have the skills to do the job? It   might not be to the same standard, and they might need to ask for help along the way, but could they have a go?
- Could a task be broken into smaller, bite-sized chunks and parts of it allocated to others? Let's use a basic household example. Your small child may not be able to operate the washing machine, but they could sort the washing into piles of lights and darks, and put it into the machine, ready for you to programme and start it.
- Is this a regular task that you have to do quite often? If so, it's an ideal task to delegate, as you'll only have to show someone how to do it once and then they'll be able to take ownership.

If you've decided to go ahead and delegate, make sure you explain the job well to the person you're handing the job over to. Be patient, as it may take them a little while to get comfortable with it, and support them along the way. You won't regret it and will see your To Do list become more manageable as a result.

We've now covered most of the theory of Time Management. Make sure you check out the resources section to find additional help and here's some final tips about how to work more effectively and efficiently:

- Try not to pick up a job, start it and then put it back on the pile. You should only handle a task once. Pick it up and complete it before moving on to something else.
- Make sure your work area is tidy. This is as important at home as it is at work. I'm a big fan of de-cluttering, and it's for a very good reason. Mess makes it difficult to see things clearly and to be organised.

- If you're getting interrupted whilst working on tasks, try and go somewhere quiet. Again, this is as important at home as it is at work. I've had to go and sit in my car at times, just so I can concentrate and get on with something with no disruptions.

So, let's get started with seeing how Microsoft® Outlook can help us apply these strategies and get ourselves streamlined and organised to free up that valuable time.

Familiarising Yourself with The Outlook Screen

29

Microsoft® Outlook

So, we're ready to look at how Microsoft® Outlook can help use the skills and strategies we've covered in the previous chapters. The version of Microsoft® Outlook referred to throughout this book is 2016 for Windows but the tools we examine are available in the 2007 software onwards, and are similar to the Microsoft® Outlook for Mac version too. In fact, you'll find comparable tools in a wide range of email software, not just Microsoft® Outlook, and also apps for phones and tablets, such as those that work with calendars, tasks or reminders.

If you're very familiar with Microsoft® Outlook, particularly version 2016, you may want to skip this chapter which is absolutely fine (hey, you'd be practising prioritisation!). But if not sure, it's worth joining me to familiarise yourself with the program and main screens. That way, you'll feel more comfortable and confident when moving around the different elements of the application examined in subsequent chapters.

Let's start by talking about what Microsoft® Outlook is. Well, it has many purposes. It's an email program, a calendar which enables us to schedule appointments and meetings, an address book for keeping safe everyone's contact details, a planner for our tasks and To Do lists and there's even a notes feature too, allowing us to jot down all those important things to remember. This book focusses on emails, the calendar and tasks but we'll have a quick look at contacts too.

Please don't feel that Microsoft® Outlook is only useful if you're working, and in a busy role, with hundreds of emails coming in each day, and lots of meetings to attend. It's helpful for working in any role, and for using at home too particularly if you have to multi-task.

So, let's have a look at the Microsoft® Outlook window.

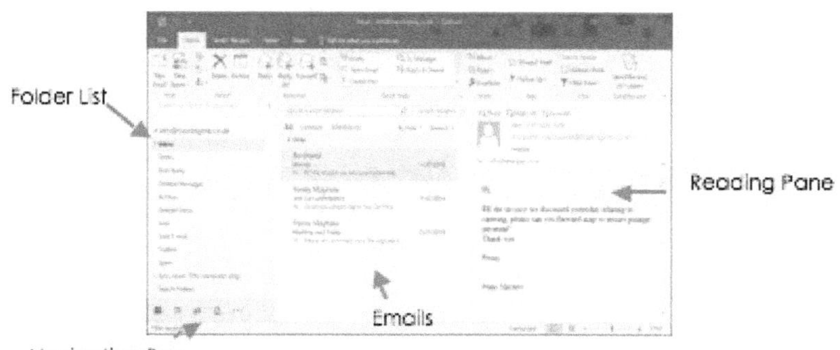

You'll see the screen is separated into columns from left to right. The default is that it opens in the Mail view, although this can be changed to open to a different part of Microsoft® Outlook if you'd prefer (you can do this via Options which is accessed by clicking the File tab to take you to the Backstage View). The email folders are shown down the left hand side in a folder pane, with emails then displayed in the next column. And, if you have the reading pane activated, this will show either on the right, or, underneath (see next chapter). At the bottom of the folder list we have the navigation bar and this allows us to move around the different features of Microsoft® Outlook such as Mail, Calendar etc. You'll see the main screen change as you click onto the different icons.

At the top of the screen we have the tabs and ribbons, and these change depending on which part of Microsoft® Outlook you are using at the time. For example, the Home ribbon will show you actions to carry out on emails whilst in the Mail view, but will change to Calendar actions if you swap to the Calendar part of Microsoft® Outlook.

So, let's have a look at each of the screens in more detail. We won't cover the tools quite yet, but we'll become more familiar with what's offered by the different parts of Microsoft Outlook to help us organise and manage our time better.

The Mail Screen

Let's start with finding out more about the Mail view.

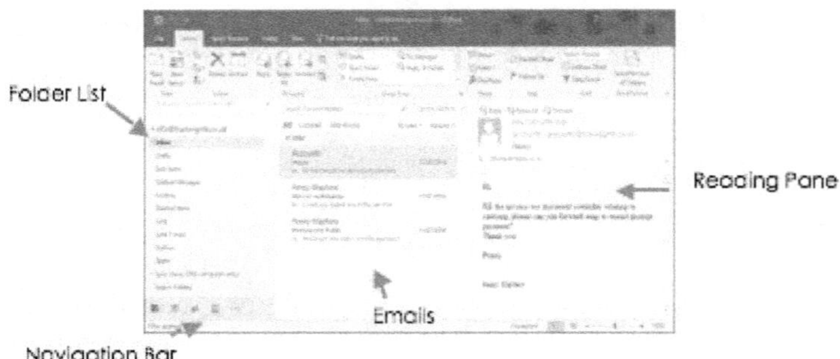

This part of the application allows us to send and receive email messages and attachments, and keep them organised so that we can find them when needed. You'll see that Mail shows quite a lot of folders in the folder pane on the left hand side, such as the Inbox which is where new messages are received.

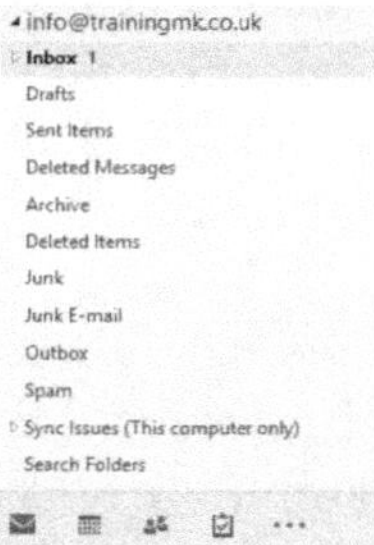

And, if any messages have not yet been read, a number appears next to the folder name to show how many are waiting for you.

The main screen shows you a list of email messages that are either read or unopened. You're able to read a message by selecting it in the list and then using the Reading Pane to view it. Or, you can double click the message to open it in its own window, whichever suits you best. However, using the one-click method is a time saver – if you double click the message to read it in its own window, you'll have to close it again when you're finished. With the one-click method, you just select another message in the list to move on.

The **Reading Pane** can be placed to the right of the email list, or below it. This is down to your own personal preference although you'll see in later chapters that having it below the list can give you more options when it comes to managing your emails.

To change the position of the Reading Pane:

- Go to the View ribbon and select the Reading Pane icon

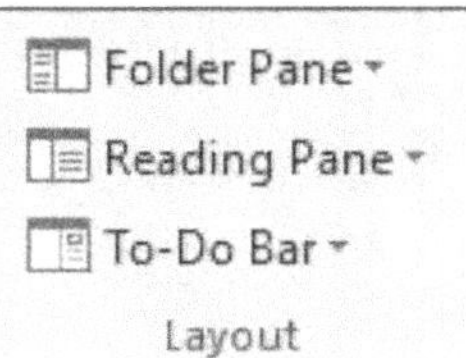

- Click to change to the required position

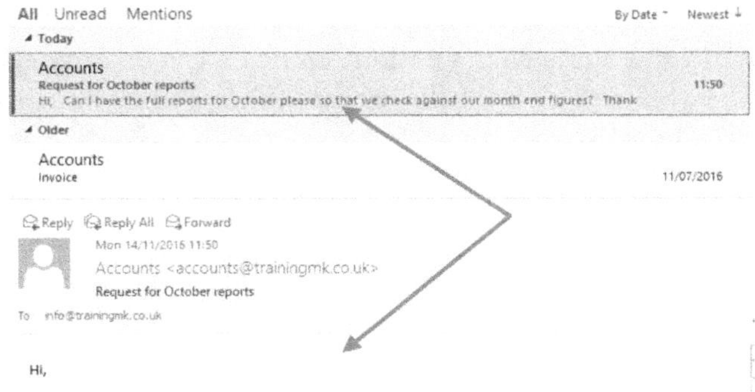

You can also add the To Do pane on the right hand side and the icon for switching is on and off is in the same group as the Reading Pane. This is a very useful feature and we'll be looking at it later. To display it:

- Go to the View ribbon and click the To Do Bar icon
- Add the elements you require. The Calendar will be displayed along with any upcoming appointments you might have, and the Task pane will show you any pending tasks.

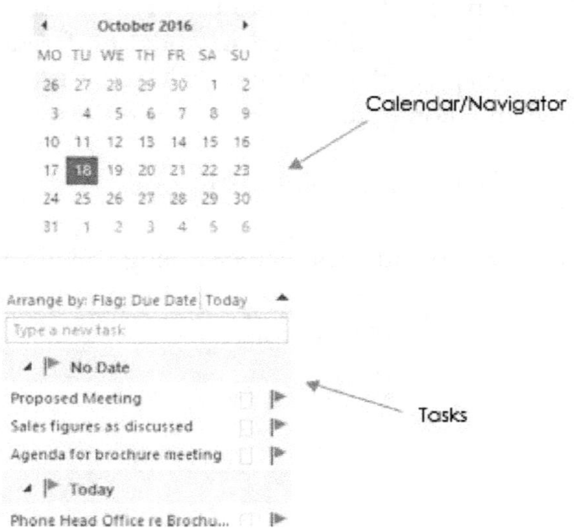

We'll look more at emails later as there are many features that integrate with the Time Management tactics we've examined. But for now, let's have a quick look around the other screens within Microsoft® Outlook.

The Calendar Screen

We'll now take a quick peek at the Calendar view. You can get to the Calendar by clicking on the icon in the Navigation bar at the bottom of the screen.

The Calendar is a great help in keeping you organised. It allows you to create appointments, meetings and jobs to do. Depending on the view you choose it gives you an opportunity to really keep on top of everything, and all that multi-tasking that you regularly do, whether at work or home.

Calendar in
Month View

The views available to you when working with the Calendar are day view, work week (omitting Saturdays and Sundays), full week or month. Your choice will depend on the amount of detail you want to be able to see. I quite like swapping to the month view to see the 'big picture', and how my things are mapping out in terms of availability. But to view my days and week in more detail, I would swap to one of the other views. You can change the view by using the icons on the Home ribbon.

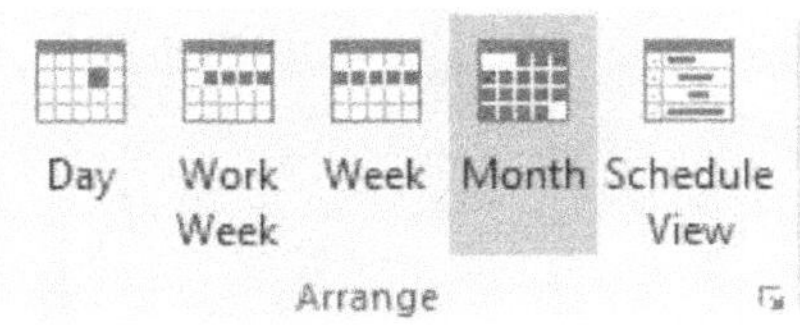

Remember too that the Calendar will be displayed, along with any upcoming appointments, if you've chosen to view the To Do bar whilst working in Mail view. This is great when you don't want to lose focus on what needs to be done whilst you're in the Mail screen.

You will also get a quick glimpse of the calendar if you hover over the Calendar icon in the navigation bar.

You'll see when we cover the Calendar in more detail later that it allows us to really think about our time and how we manage it. Once time has been scheduled into the Calendar it's much easier to commit to achieving all the things you need to do. For some reason, if we see it in our calendar (or a diary) we feel more obliged to deal with it!

Let's now take a quick look at Contacts. We don't really focus too much on Contacts during this book but it's another handy area of Outlook that can help you manage your time. There's quick ways of communicating with people...

The Contacts Screen

Using Contacts in Microsoft® Outlook lets you keep information about 'people' all in one place. It's like an address book on steroids as it allows you to collate far more information like people's birthdays, website, anniversaries – even their dog's name if you want to! Even though this isn't really connected to the Time Management skills we've discussed so far, keeping data organised and in one place is time efficient, logical and saves you vital minutes when trying to remember important information.

To access the Contacts area of Microsoft® Outlook just click the icon on the navigation bar.

Any contacts stored will be shown. To add a new contact, click the New Contact icon on the Home tab.

You'll see a form to complete.

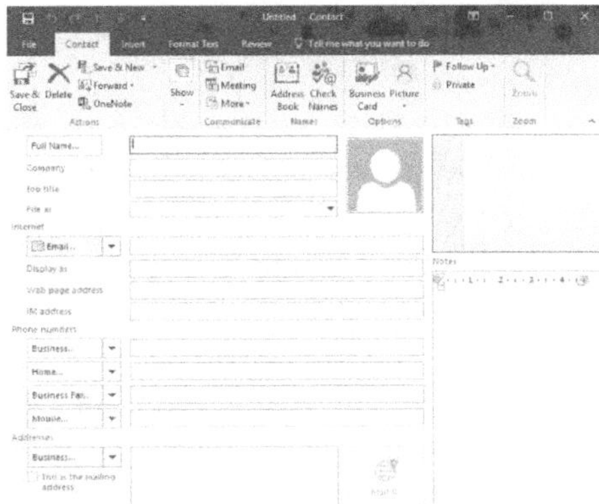

Look at all the information you can enter! Several of the fields have a button you can click to open up further options, such as Full Name which will allow you to include a title, middle name etc.

Use the Notes field on the Contact screen to record as much information as you can, such as how you know them, points of interest, small details that you might need in the future but would take a long time to find if written on notes or the back of an envelope somewhere.

And, just in case you're planning on visiting your contact and are not quite sure of the way, you can click the 'Map It' icon in the Contact's window. As long as you're connected to the Internet, the web browser opens with a map showing their address right in the centre. (Note: Make sure you have an email address for them in the stored Contact, as it needs this to work.)

Once you've filled out the necessary fields, click 'Save & Close'. You'll see the contacts stored alphabetically. To open up a contact to view information, or to edit, double click the name in the list, make the edits and then save and close.

So how else can we make even more effective use of Contacts in terms of Time Management? Well, you can go straight to emailing a contact from the screen by clicking the icon.

This saves you from coming away from Contacts back to the email screen, then opening a new email and addressing it to your contact. Clicking the icon will take you straight to an email message with their name already entered in the To field.

And, if you receive an email from someone that's not in your contact list, simply right-click their name in the email message window and select 'Add to Outlook Contacts' from the shortcut menu.

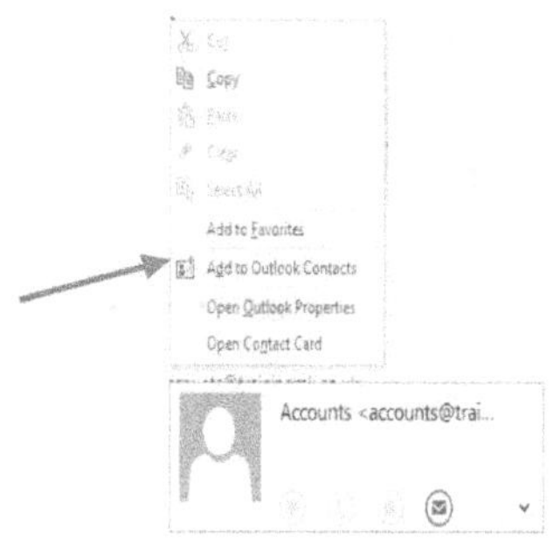

Next, we'll look at the Task window, an area with many tools and functionality to help keep you super organised!

The Tasks Screen

The last main screen we'll look at is the Tasks area of Microsoft® Outlook. We'll be visiting this a lot during the later chapters as Tasks relate to so many of the Time Management strategies we've already examined, and so this is just a little insight into how the feature works.

If ever I start to feel overwhelmed by the amount of work I have to do, and am forgetting important things, it's always because, for some reason, I've stopped using a To Do list. We've covered the importance of creating a To Do list in an earlier chapter - it will make you feel more focused and organised, whilst also helping to prioritise and plan your time better in order to be more effective. As much as we'd like to think we can remember everything, and carry all of those things to do around in our head, the truth is it just doesn't work. And, even though paper 'To Do' lists help to some extent, they can become lost, often buried at the bottom of a bag or drawer. Tasks in Microsoft® Outlook is one of the electronic tools you can use to get your To Do lists well and truly sorted.

The idea of the Tasks area in Microsoft® Outlook is to show you what needs to be done and when. Click the Tasks icon on the navigation bar at the bottom of the screen.

You'll see the window is mainly taken up by an area which displays any tasks you've created clearly along with deadlines (if you've chosen to set them). They'll even appear in red when overdue.

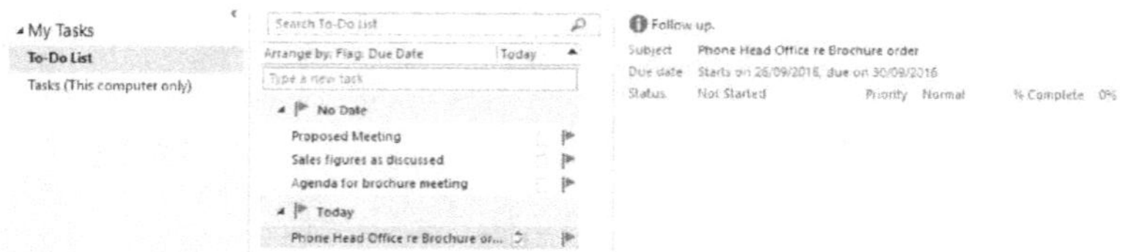

Just like emails, you can use the Reading Pane to display everything about the task. To display the Reading Pane:

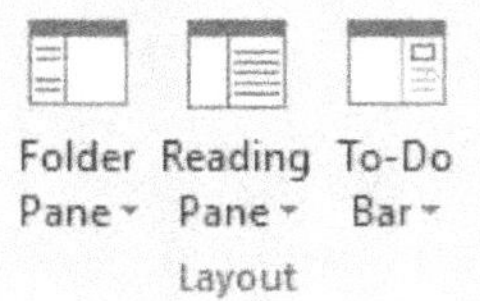

*   Go to the View tab and click the Reading Pane icon
*   Choose whether to show it on the right, or below

You can view your tasks in different ways, such as a To Do list, and they can be filtered to show those that are overdue or that are due in the next few days. This helps keep you focussed. You can change the view by going to the View Ribbon and choosing the most appropriate icon in the Arrangement group.

Tasks can have files attached to them which makes it easy to keep everything together in one place, and you can set reminders, just in case you might forget that important thing to do. Of course, the reminders can be dismissed or set to snooze, and can be ignored totally by closing a reminder message. But, this would be procrastinating, and we've already talked about that...

We'll be covering tasks in much more detail throughout the book as they're a vital element of how we can use Microsoft® Outlook to help us manage our time. Now we're going to really get started! We're going to first look at something we do probably every day – send emails. Are you using all the features that can help you manage your time better? Let's see!

Getting Your Emails Under Control

Stop Bothering Me!

It doesn't matter how organised you are, there's one sure distraction that will stop you in your tracks. emails! If Microsoft® Outlook (or any other email program) is open whilst you're trying to get on with things, it's almost guaranteed that you'll be tempted to check your email literally every few minutes. It's irresistible! And then, before you know it, you'll be answering an email, and then another will come in, and so you'll answer that one, etc. etc. In the blink of an eye half an hour has passed and you've got absolutely no-where. So, what can you do about it?

Well, there's a few things that can help, but you've got to be tough and make sure you do them. Remember what I said right at the start – you have to commit to change or else things will continue exactly as they are.

The first thing you can do is to put a curfew on yourself in terms of checking emails. Set yourself key times throughout the day. If you're at work, plan in time to check your email first thing, then at lunchtime, and then half an hour before you leave for the day. That way, you'll be able to stay uninterrupted during the rest of the time and will be flying through that list of jobs. You're probably thinking, 'but hey, what if something urgent comes in?' Unless you're in a job where you have a set time limit on how long you can leave it before responding to an email, it can wait a few hours. If you absolutely have to, add in a quick check mid-morning and afternoon, say around 11am and 2:30pm. You'll then have at least 90 minutes or so uninterrupted. And remember, they'll ring if it's mega urgent, or, come to find you.

If it's still too irresistible then shut down Microsoft® Outlook during the hours where you've committed to not check your emails. I know, scary right? You'll cope... and It will stop you being tempted.

But, if you have to keep it switched on, then there's one further thing you can do to try to stop the temptation to click on that email icon every few minutes. Turn off the Desktop Alert! It's the little message that fades in subtly at the bottom of the screen when an email arrives. It will tell you the sender, the subject and a short preview of the message which of course, if you see it, you'll want to open and respond. So, turn it off to resist that temptation! Just think, every time you scan over the image as it appears on your screen, you're losing track of where you are with the job you're working on, and then you have to spend seconds to get tuned back in. All of those seconds add up!

To turn off the Desktop Alert:

- Go to the File tab and select Options

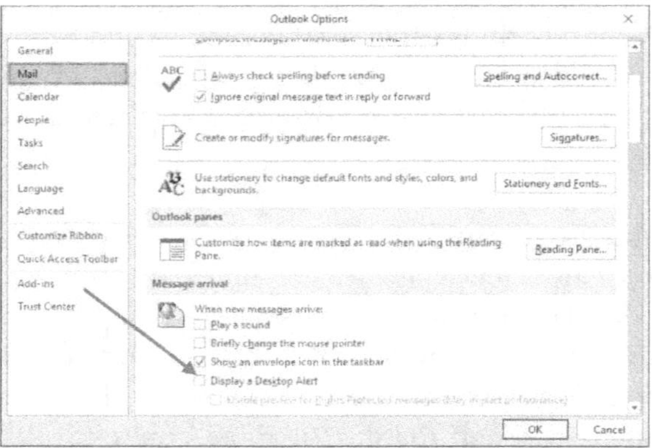

- In the 'Message Arrival' section, select or clear the 'Display a Desktop Alert' check box

This chapter is more about incoming emails. But, what about the ones you're sending? Are you spending your time productively? Is an email the best form of communication, or the most appropriate? Or is it another way of procrastinating and avoiding a difficult task? Let's take a look!

To Send or Not To Send?

As email can be one of our top time thieves it's very important to ensure that you've actually chosen the most appropriate method of communication. Before investing your precious time in creating an email, ask yourself 'Is this the best way of delivering the message?' In other words, have you considered the alternatives?

We all get too many emails and many that we receive should never have been sent in the first place. If you have a simple question, or a simple response, then emailing fits the bill. Someone needs a document? Great, attach it to an email message and they'll receive it within minutes compared to days if having to post. That's pretty obvious and an easy choice to make. But, let's look at when it's not such a good idea.

Firstly, can you think of a time when you received an email and felt either offended, annoyed, confused or upset? There's very few people that haven't experienced this at some time or another, whether at home or work. It's difficult to convey the intended tone when we write an email and just one word can be enough to spark a whole range of problems. When we read an email we can't hear the person's voice and so can interpret an intended joke or light hearted comment as being negative and accusing. And, don't presume that putting a smiley face emoji at the end of a sentence or phrase will save you. Instead, it can add to someone's frustration!

Think of the time that's then needed to try and diffuse the situation if it occurs; the further emails to patch things up, the awkward phone call, the visit to apologise. Try to minimise the risks so that it doesn't happen in the first place.

So, when is it not appropriate to send emails? Well, there's no point in sending someone a message to cancel a meeting just 15 minutes before it's due to go ahead. Not everyone will read their emails whilst on their way to, or at the start of, a meeting and could be then sat waiting for you to attend without even knowing it's cancelled. If you need to cancel at the last minute, use the telephone to speak to someone directly.

If you need something done straight away, don't send an email to ask someone. They might not read it for a while, or understand the urgency, and it's not fair to then get annoyed with them. It's down to you, for not having rung them instead, or gone to see them. Actually, question yourself if sending an email like this, where you're asking a person to do something straight away. Make sure it's not because you don't feel assertive enough to ask them face to face or over the telephone.

What about those long emails you receive, which go on and on... Lengthy and complex matters are not meant for emails. They become confusing when lengthy and offer no opportunity for the recipient to ask questions or for you, the sender, to confirm the message has been understood.

And a final example is when we have bad news to break. When there's a difficult conversation to be had, an email is not an appropriate method of communication. It should take place face to face or, if absolutely necessary, by telephone. If you find yourself writing an email of this nature, think again...

Now, wouldn't it be lovely if we could ask Microsoft® Outlook to send any replies to our emails directly to someone else instead? Well, we can. Let's see how!

I Nominate You!

So, this is a little more relevant for emailing in the workplace rather than at home. Let's imagine that you're sending out an email to several people about an event that's going to be taking place which you're coordinating or managing. You need the recipients to reply to your message but, as soon as you've hit that send icon, you're going to be off and out of the building, rushing away on your long awaited holiday.

Now, it doesn't matter how much you state the fact you're going to be away in the body text of the email, and that they need to reply to your colleague, the recipients are busy people too, just like you, and are likely to still hit that Reply button. You'll return from your wonderful 2 weeks on the beach, only to be faced with a load of unread messages waiting for you, some of which are now out of date and no longer relevant because the message needed to be actioned during the last 14 days. So what can you do?

Well, Microsoft® Outlook has a neat little option that lets you nominate other people to automatically receive the reply. It doesn't actually need to be a different person as such, as you may, for example, want the replies to go to your personal email address rather than your work email. Think of the time this would save? You wouldn't have to spend time logging into your work account and clicking Forward for each message (hey, we know what happens if we log into our work account whilst on holiday - before you know it, you're clicking on messages, replying, forwarding and, basically, working! So, I'm not a big advocate of this.)

To nominate another person to receive the reply:

- In the message you're sending, go to the Options ribbon

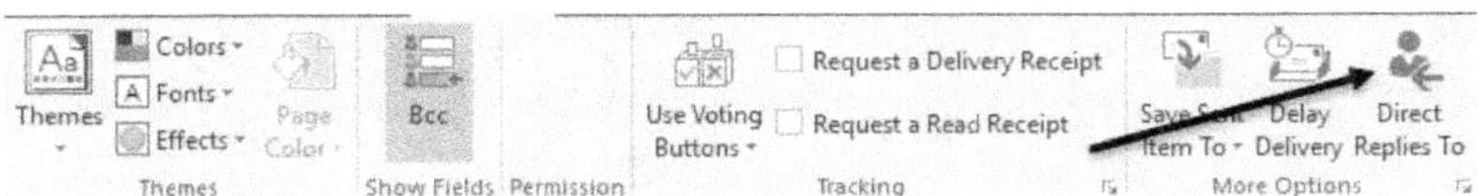

- Click the 'Direct Replies To' icon. This will take you to the Options dialog box:

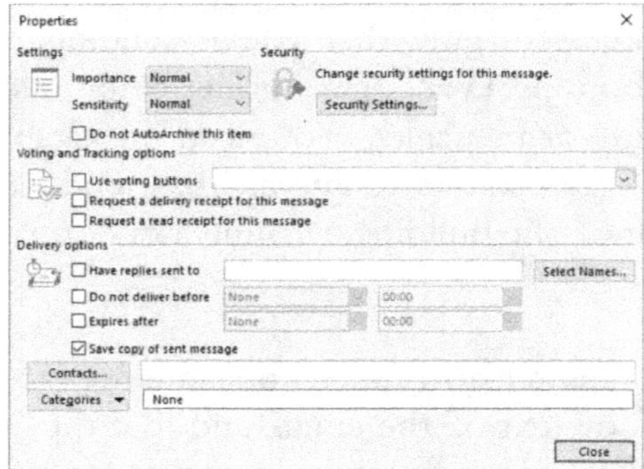

- Under Delivery Options, make sure the check box is selected and then type the address of a recipient in the 'Have replies sent to' field alongside, or, click the Select Names button to choose from the address list.
- Click Close

There... any replies will now go to the nominated person. Now, before you get too carried away, always make sure you've let the nominated person know! You need their permission or else you'll arrive back and be faced by a very angry colleague.

This is a great example of delegation which we mentioned in one of the earlier chapters. If you haven't time to do a job, or you're not able to do it for whatever reason, see if someone else can help.

Next we'll look at how we can delay the delivery of email messages so that they leave our Outbox at a specified date and time.

Not Quite Ready...

Another really useful feature of Microsoft® Outlook is that it allows you to delay the delivery of an email message. This is a great way to help with Time Management.

For example, let's say you have five really important email messages to send out on a Friday afternoon but, the way the week is going, you know you'll be so busy when the time comes that there's a danger you'll forget. One option is that you could write the emails earlier in the week, whilst you have a bit of time on your hands, and then save them into the draft folder. All you'll then need to do on Friday afternoon is go into the emails when it's time and click the Send button. But, the reason you're having to do this is because you're going to be very busy on Friday afternoon, so there's a very good chance you'll forget to press send when the time comes. Or maybe you're not going to be near the computer at the set time anyway.

Let Microsoft® Outlook do the hard work for you...

To delay the delivery of a message:

- In the email message you are going to send, click the Options tab and select 'Delay Delivery'

- This takes you to the Options dialog box. Make sure the 'Do Not Deliver Before' check box is selected and then set the Delivery date and time

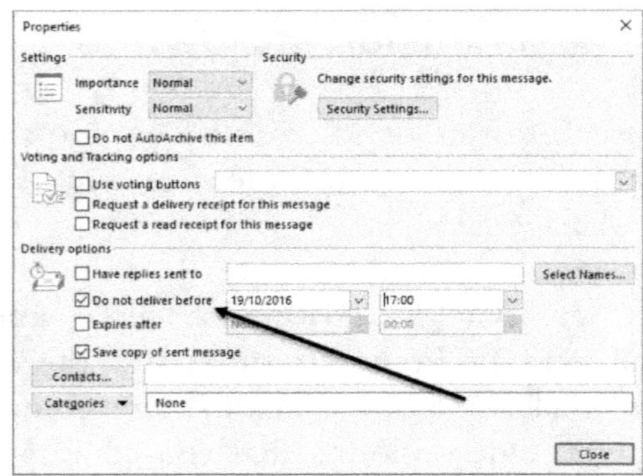

- Click Close

The email message, or messages, will then sit in your Outbox until the designated date and time arrives. Then, they will go smoothly out of your mailbox en-route to the recipient, just like that! The message can be ticked off in your To Do list and forgotten about, leaving you free to deal with your most vital tasks.

In the next chapter we'll look at how we can make an email message into a task – this is a great way of remembering that an email needs some sort of action, as it will show up in two places; the To Do Bar within your email screen and Tasks.

Don't Forget Me!

When we're busy either at work or home we often find ourselves multi-tasking. We're doing our chores, answering calls, liaising with different people, working on documents and files, and keeping an eye on emails coming in. We catch sight of a message and vow to respond a little later, when it's less busy. Except, it rarely becomes 'less busy'. So, the email gets buried in our Inbox and potentially could be forgotten about.

Now, tasks are covered in a different chapter and we'll learn all about them there, but this is a quick feature that can really help you keep on top of those important emails. Forget about writing yourself a note to remember to respond later, or even setting a reminder on your Smart Phone or Tablet app. Let Microsoft Outlook turn the email into a task, adding it automatically to your To Do list which is viewable on the email screen. There's then less chance of it being forgotten. And, the added bonus is that you get to tick it as complete once done.

To make your email message into a task, you simply:

- Select the email in the inbox
- On the right hand side of the message, click the small flag

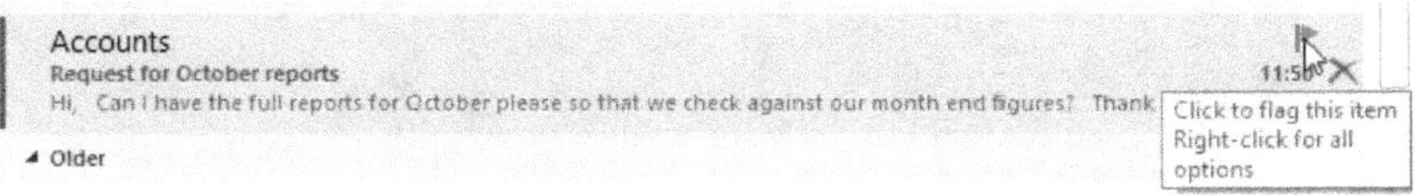

- This will place a red flag next to the email and it will also show in your To Do Bar

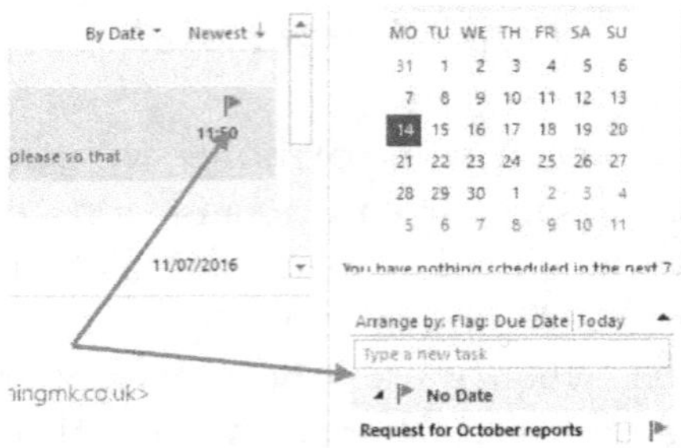

Once you are ready to deal with the email, you can either open it from the Inbox or from the To Do Bar (by double clicking). This prevents you having to look around a cluttered folder, saving vital time and energy. You can then click the flag to show it as complete.

We'll cover Tasks in much more detail later in the book. We're now ready to move onto our next section where we're going to tackle that misbehaving Inbox. Let's get organised!

De-clutter that inbox

Let's Get Filing!

How organised are you in general? Are you 'clutter free' or do you store things absolutely anywhere in the home or office and just hope for the best when it's time to find them quickly? It's easy to let things build up, and an unstructured and unorganised life style can have a real effect on not only our Time Management, but on stress levels too. We can lose minutes and even hours looking for important documents, keys, the phone etc. and, each time it happens, we vow to get tidier. But then it happens again... Clutter is another time thief!

Imagine having a big cardboard box in your lounge that sits on a table. Every-time you receive a letter or document in the post, you throw it in. Over time, the pile grows higher and higher, with no structure to it at all. So, when you need to find something, you have to search through the whole box. Imagine instead a filing cabinet, with several drawers, all grouped alphabetically. So maybe the top drawer is anything filed under the letters A to G, the second drawer down under the letters H to P etc. Inside each drawer is another filing structure, with folders hanging in suspension files. Each of the suspension files has a tab on the top showing exactly what's in there, and it's in alphabetical order. How easy it is to both file and find letters and documents!

This is the environment we need to create in our email Inbox. By default, as soon as an email arrives it goes into the Inbox folder and after sending an email, once it leaves the Outbox, it is saved in the Sent Items folder. If we leave the emails there, it's the same as using the big cardboard box on the table in the lounge. It will soon come cluttered and fit to burst. But we can make it much more organised, particularly if you receive lots of emails every day. You could create a folder in the Inbox relating to a particular project, for example, or for a person or group that you regularly communicate with. Then, you can move any message, whether received or sent, into that folder for easier retrieval later.

To create a new folder:

- Go to the Folder tab and click the New Folder icon

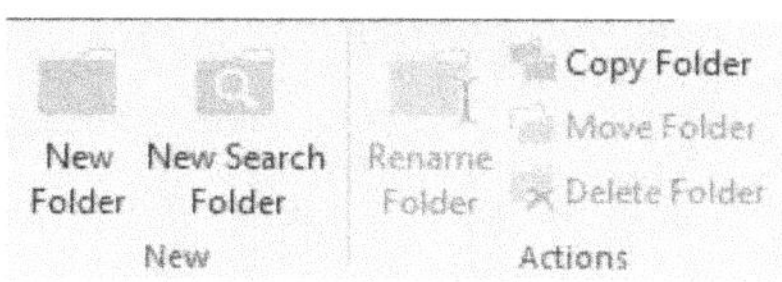

- Type a name for the folder and select its location. You may want to place it into the Inbox but there could be a folder within the Inbox which would act better as the Parent folder. For example, a folder in the Inbox could be called Team, and you want to create a folder for each team member within the Team folder

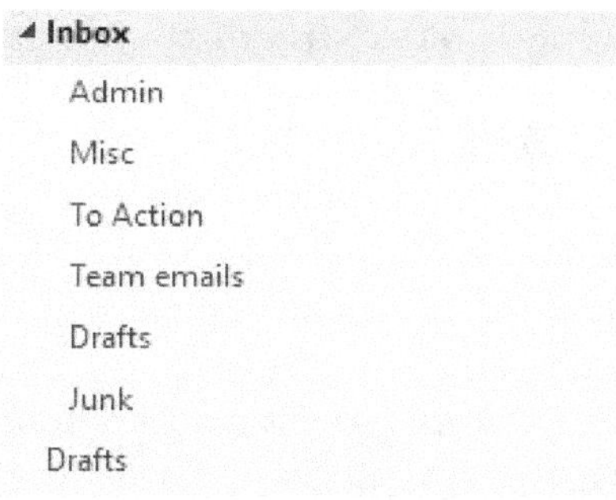

- Click OK

Or, why not use the right-click method. Just right-click a folder in the Inbox and select New Folder, enter a name and press Enter.

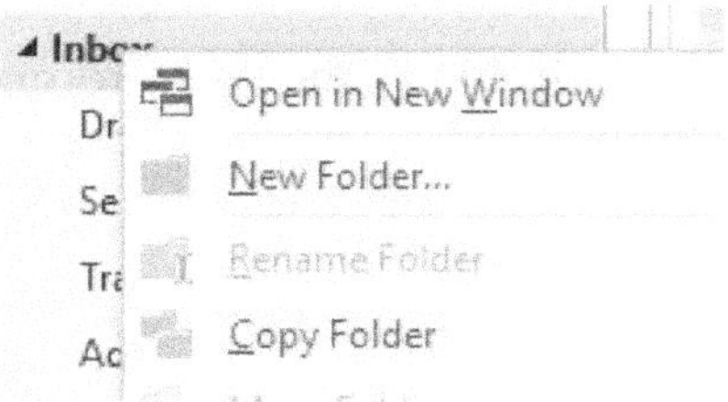

If you've made a folder in error, or no longer need it, you can select it and then, on the Folder tab, click Delete Folder.

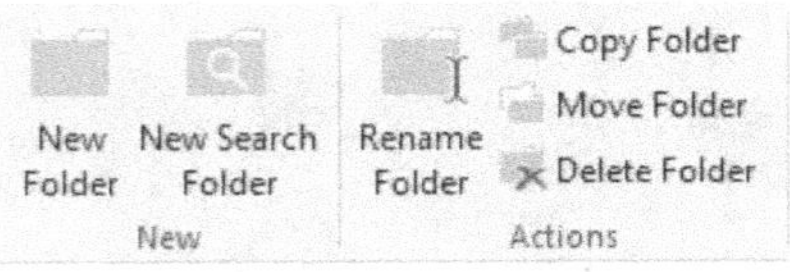

Or, right click the folder and Delete. (You can rename it too with a right click or via the Folder tab.)

Be careful if you delete a folder though as it will also delete any messages that might be in that folder rather than spilling them back out to the Inbox or Sent Items.

Have a go at creating a folder structure – look through your emails and see what folders would be useful to have. Imagine you placing them in a physical folder or filing cabinet, how would it be organised?

So, now you have your folder structure, you can move messages around and get really tidy. There's lots of different methods to choose from, go with your own personal preference:

- Select the message in the Inbox and, on the Home tab, click the Move button

- The folder you want to move the email to may be shown in the top part of the drop down list

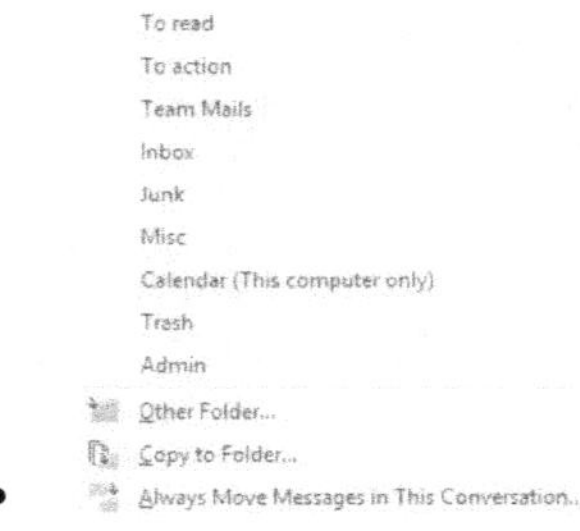

- If you do not see the Folder you require, click on Other Folder

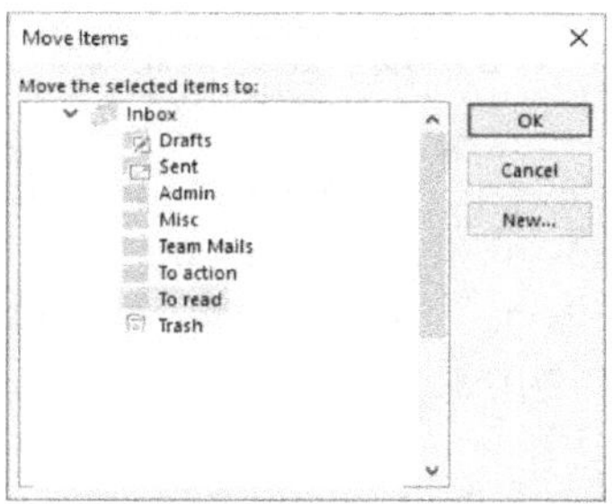

Or

- Right click the message and choose Move, then repeat as above
  Or
- Click and drag the message straight into the folder showing in the list.

So you're now set up to help banish the time thieves known as 'clutter and chaos'! So what else can we do with the Inbox?

Taming the Inbox

What can we do to make it easier to manage those emails and keep things under control? Well, going back to our Time Matrix, and how we deal with jobs we need to do, the same principals can be applied to our Inbox management.

For each message that comes in, we need to really think about what we want to do. The key is, don't ignore it and leave it sitting in that Inbox. The Inbox will quickly become full, making message retrieval difficult whilst also slowing your system down. Take a look at that message and consider the following:

- Do you need it? Many of our emails can be deleted either because they're for information only, are junk or something that's not really even meant for us. A key offender is the dreaded 'reply to all' email, the one that went out to a group and then those involved insisted on clicking 'reply to all' when their comment was only really relevant to the person who originally sent the message. If you don't need it, delete it immediately! Or, if it's from someone that's annoying you, and that keeps sending email after email, you can use the Ignore button on the Home tab which will move any current and future messages from that sender straight to the Deleted Items folder.

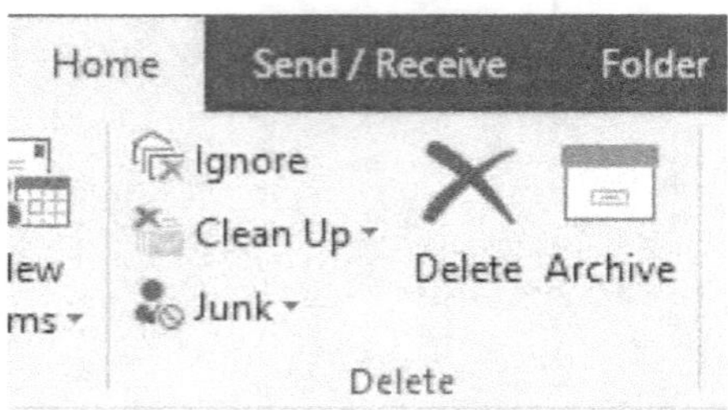

- Is it something you can action in a couple of minutes or less? Then do it! Don't put it off and think you'll do it later, because chances are you won't. If it's a quick job, then get it done and move on to the next on your list. And, when you've actioned it, don't just leave it sitting there in the Inbox. Think about what to do with it next. Do you need to keep it? No? Then delete it. If you do need to keep it, pop it into a folder you've created and keep the number of messages in your Inbox to a minimum.

*   Is it something meant for someone else to action? If so, delegate! Forward it to whoever can deal with it and get it out of that Inbox.

*   And that just leaves the messages you need to action but need longer than just a couple of minutes. Think about deferring it (such as by flagging which we covered in an earlier chapter), or maybe create a folder called 'To Action' and then return to it when you have the time.

Once your Inbox is under control you can make it even easier to view your messages by changing the way they're displayed in the Reading Pane. Check out the 'Arrange' group of icons on the View tab.

Re-ordering them by the Sender, or by the subject heading, may help you find an email more quickly than scrolling through. But if you're keeping that Inbox under control you hopefully won't need to spend lots of time finding what you're looking for.

Do you fancy learning the Quick Step! Don't worry, no dancing is involved, it's easier than you think. And you'll find out how in the next chapter.

Doing the Quick Step!

We've seen that it's pretty quick to move emails into a folder to help us get organised, but Microsoft® Outlook offers you even more help and time saving with the feature called Quick Steps. Quick Steps is located on the Home tab and there's a wide range of actions offered, such as a Quick Step to send an email to a group of people you specify, or to reply and delete a particular email all in one click. Remember, all of those clicks add up...

- On the home tab you'll see a range of default steps that can customised. Clicking 'More' will take you to further options.

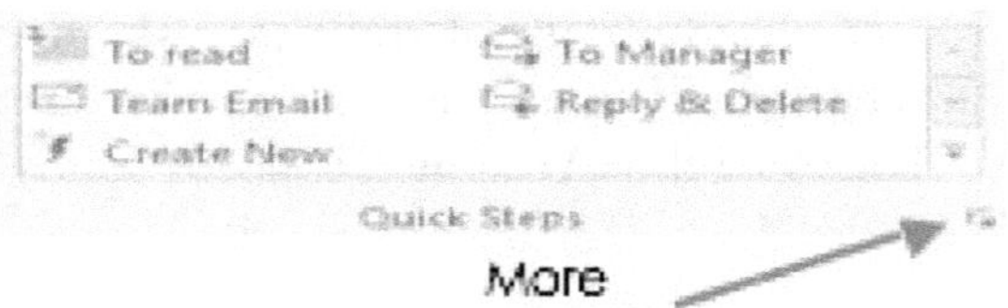

- Hover over New Quick Step to choose any of the additional Quick Steps.

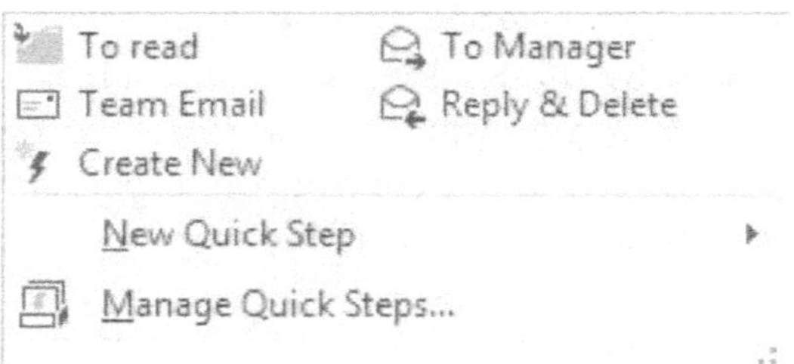

When you choose a Quick Step you will see the First Time Setup box. To create a Quick Step which moves an email automatically to a set folder:

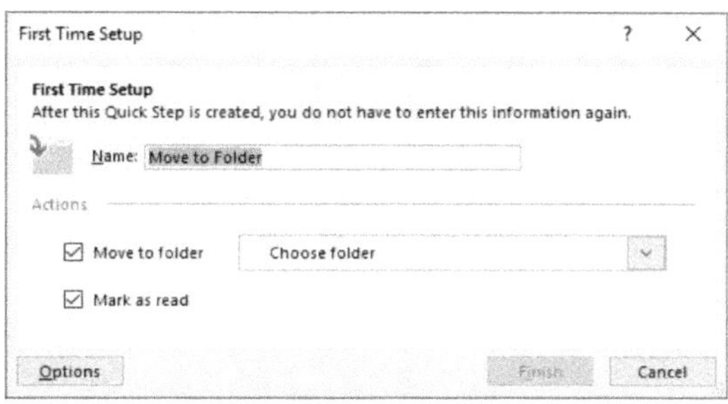

- Select the Move to Folder option
- Name the Quick Step
- Select the required folder from the Move To Folder drop down list
- Click Finish

You'll see your new Quick Step will show in the gallery on the Home tab and you'll be able to use it by just selecting a message in the Inbox and then clicking the Quick Step you've created. The message will go straight to the folder specified, as easy as that.

Check out some of the other automated Quick Steps you can use such as sending to a Team email or forwarding emails straight to a specific person, such as a manager. This can save you valuable minutes of your time and will help you work efficiently when dealing with your emails. And, if you like things in a certain order, check out the Manage Quick Steps options which allows you to rearrange them in the gallery.

Another great time-saving tool is the 'Rules' feature. Let's take a look!

Rules

A Set of Rule to Live By...

We've explored several tools and features that Microsoft® Outlook offers in terms of helping with our Time Management and keeping on top of our emails. We've seen how to create a folder structure to keep things organised, and how the Quick Steps allow us to carry out an action on an email in just one click. So, once we've either deleted, delegated or stored our emails into a folder, you should be left with a list of emails to action personally in your inbox.

But what if you could get Microsoft® Outlook to do even more for you, like carry out an administrative task automatically without needing to click a single button? Well, you can! Microsoft® Outlook can be like your own Personal Assistant, taking care of emails without even needing to bother you.

You can give Microsoft® Outlook a set of rules to live by, actions that are carried out as soon as a message either arrives or is sent, based on conditions you set. For example, as soon as you send a message to a work colleague, or a company, the sent item is moved straight into the corresponding folder.

Can you think of any automated tasks with your emails that you'd find useful? You can add as many or as few conditions and actions to a rule. And, you can add exceptions too so that it is only applied in specific circumstances. The rules can then be run either manually or automatically; the choice is entirely yours.

We're going to explore a few of the most common rules in the next few chapters, learning how to create, manage and delete them.

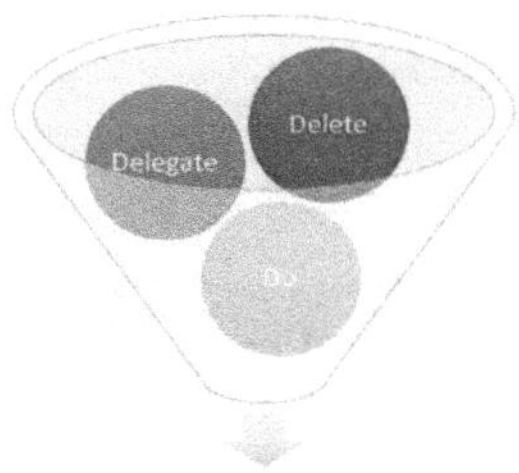

To Action

Moving Based on Content

So, Rules can perform a set of actions automatically, such as moving an email based on the content that is in the subject heading of the mail message. Think of when you could use this in terms of helping your Time Management. If you often find yourself trawling through your Inbox and moving messages one by one, this could be of real benefit.

So, how do we do it?

- First of all, go to the Home tab and click the Rules icon

- Select Manage Rules and Alerts to open the Rules Wizard
- Click the New Rule button

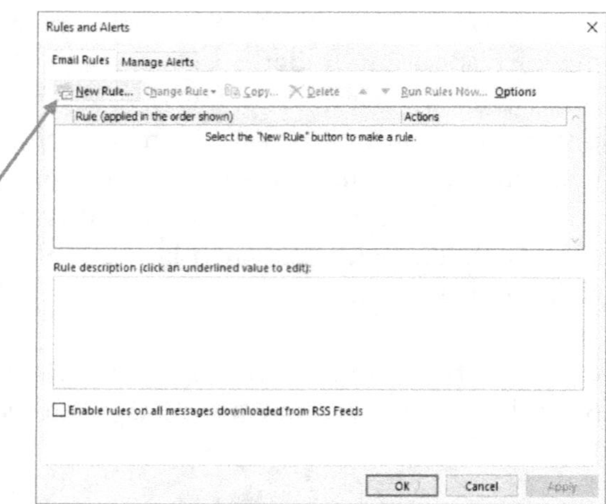

- In Step 1 click the 'Move messages with specific words in the subject to a folder'
- In step 2 click on specific words. Type the specific word(s) you want to filter by and click Add, then OK

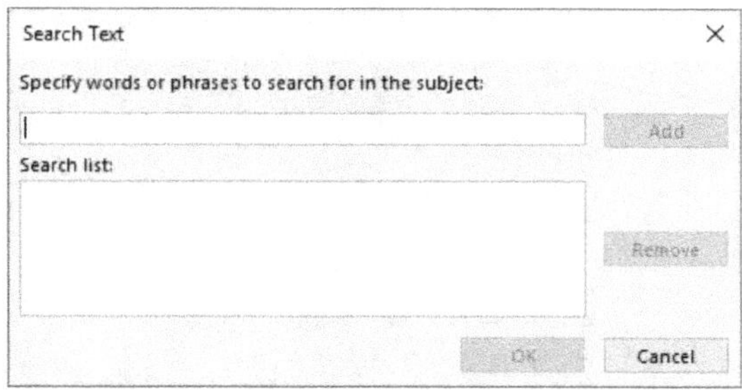

- Click on Specified folder

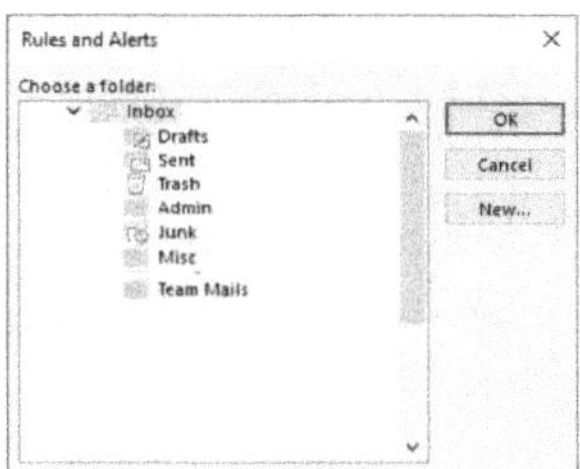

- Select an existing folder or click New to create a new folder
- Click OK
- Click Next
- Check the conditions then click Next

- Check the Actions then click Next
- Add any Exceptions if required and click Next

- Finish the rule set up by naming the Rule and confirming if you wish to turn the Rule on now and run it on the existing folders.
- Click Finish and then click OK

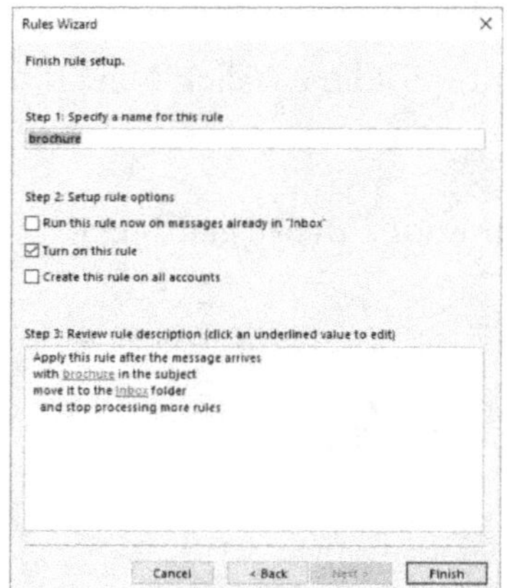

There, the rule is set ready to use! There's one more rule that's worth looking at, and that's the one that moves an email to a particular folder based on the sender, which is covered in the next chapter.

Moving Based on Sender

So, we've looked a Rule that performs an action on a message based on the subject header, and now we're going to see a Rule that sends a message to a specific folder based on the Sender. This is really useful, as it saves you having to manually drag or move a message, or multiple mails, and is really quick to do.

Before starting the Rules wizard, select an email in your Inbox which is from the Sender that you want to create the Rule for. Then, once the Rules wizard is activated, select 'Always move Messages from' in the first step. The sender should already be shown as you had selected an email from them before entering the wizard. Select the specific folder and click OK.

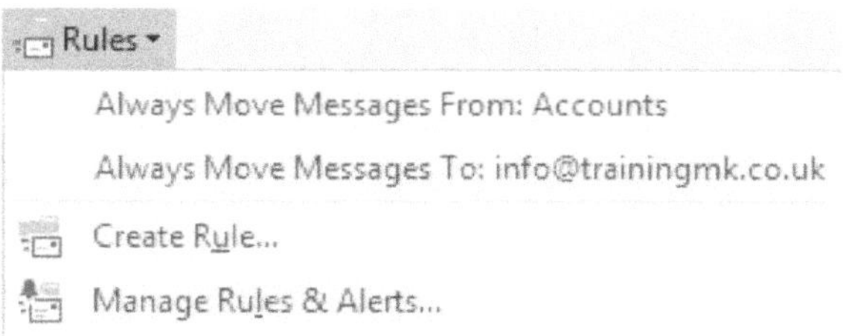

If you don't currently have an email in your Inbox that is from the required sender, you can still create the rule quite easily. When you click on the Rules icon, select Manage Rules and Alerts. This then lets you click onto New Rule, where the wizard will open.

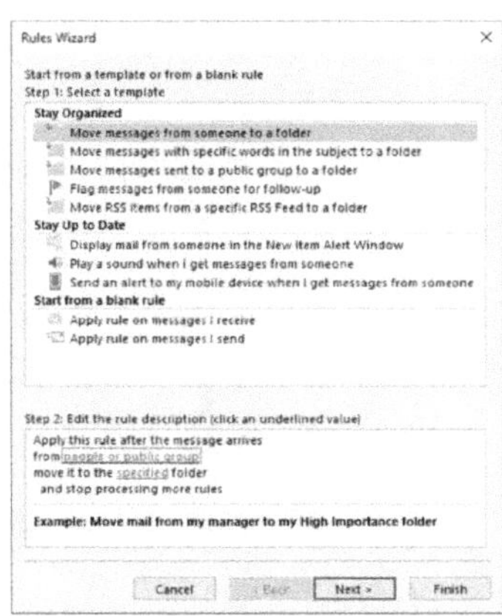

- In the Step 2 area at the bottom of the dialog box click the 'people or public group' link and either select the name or type it into the From field
- Click OK
- Specify the folder, conditions, actions or exceptions before finishing the rule set up

Have a look at your own Inbox and think about what Rules would help you keep organised. You can make as many as you want, and can even run them on the emails already in the Inbox - it's not just for new ones. But, what if you want to edit a rule, rename or delete? Is it straight forward? You bet - even though Rules help us to be more organised, having unnecessary ones just make your screen and time-saving toolbox cluttered and busy.

Renaming Rules

So, you've set up your rules and they're keeping your messages under control, minimising the time it takes to carry out general housekeeping on your Inbox. So, that's it, right? Well, not quite. Rules can get a little out of control if you let them take over. They need to be maintained and kept in check. For example, you may no longer need some of the rules you have, or the names are not specific enough and causes confusion when trying to work out which is which. Let's look at how we can tame them!

It makes sense to name a rule clearly so that it's easy to identify what the action will be just from the title. You can edit a name at any time and it will not change the Rule properties.

To rename a rule:

- Go to the Home tab and click the Rules icon
- Select Manage Rules and Alerts

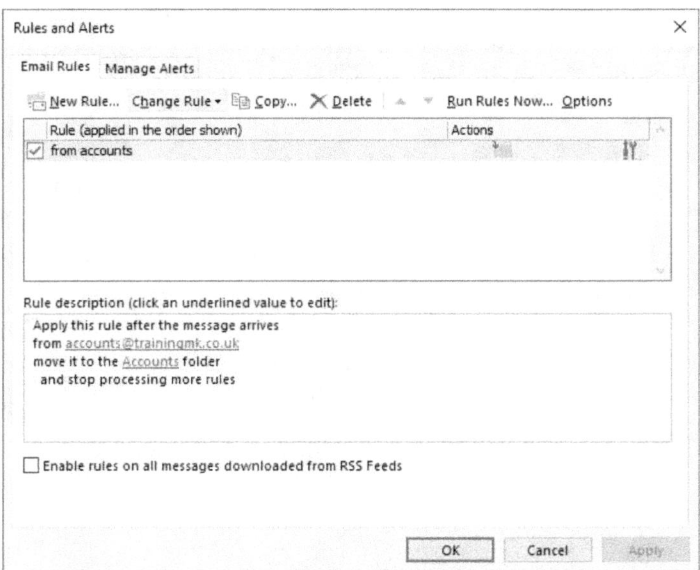

- Select the Rule that you wish to modify
- Select Change Rule

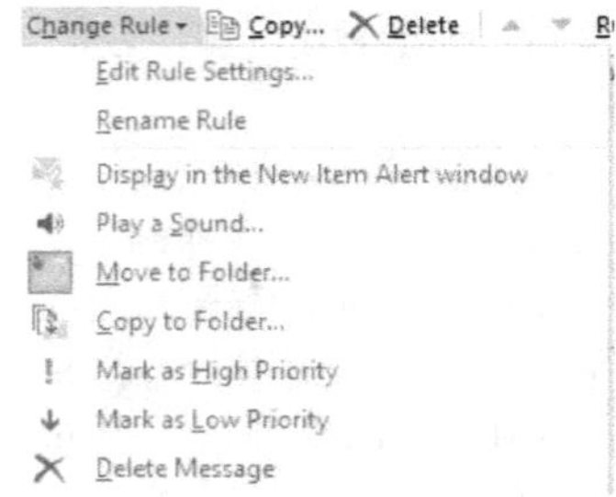

- Select Rename Rule

The only other thing you might want to do is delete a Rule. Maybe they're not necessary anymore and there's just no need to have them there, cluttering up your list. Yes, you can just turn a rule off (when you click to edit the rule in the Manage Rules window but they'll just sit there clogging up space. So, if it's no longer needed, delete and de-clutter!

To delete a Rule:

- Go to the Home tab and click the Rules icon
- Select Manage Rules and Alerts
- Select the Rule you wish to modify
- Click Delete

There, you're all set to work with Rules and get those emails under control! Remember that tidiness and organisation are key to managing time and an untidy Inbox will make those important emails difficult to find. It's time to get tough!

So, we're now ready to start exploring the Calendar and to revisit some of the Time Management techniques we covered in the first few chapters.

What's In Your Calendar?

Scheduling Time For You

The calendar in Microsoft® Outlook is often under-utilised whether using it at home or work. In particular, many work-users only go into the calendar to book meetings but it can be so much more useful than that. It should contain the jobs you need to do, and tasks or projects you are working on, so that your time is protected. If others are looking at your calendar (this is more common in the work environment but it's possible to share a calendar with others at home) they need to be able to see when you are committed so that they don't pinch the time from you. Remember the time thieves! It's easy to drop everything as soon as someone asks you to because we are generally polite and want to help where we can. But, if it's in the calendar, that time is yours. Other people don't have to know the ins and outs of your commitment, they just need to understand that you're busy. And so do you! It's ourselves that we need to convince as much as other people.

It's really important to remember that in addition to the time you need to allocate to complete the actual jobs themselves, you also need to set time aside to spend on planning and reflection. If you don't do this, then you will find it hard to properly manage your To Do list, and all the work you need to get through. Also, don't miss out those 'jobs' that you consider as miscellaneous tasks, such as phone calls you need to make or face to face visits. If you don't schedule these in, you'll run out of time as other things will take priority. This 'planning' time should be scheduled as regular appointments in your calendar. Once the job is planned, it's easier to commit to achieving the task at the right time. Refer back to that time matrix we covered earlier in the course – which of those tasks could be scheduled in your calendar?

Set time aside to:

- Deal with your emails. This is very important, particularly if you receive a lot and they need to be dealt with in a timely manner. 15 minutes first thing in the morning could be enough to go through those messages that have come in overnight, even if it's just to prioritise, delegate or delete. Use the tools we covered in the email section to sort, organise and prioritise those mail messages. Then, you can start your day fresh.

- Review your tasks and appointments. Check them in terms of prioritisation and use the time matrix to decide which are both urgent and important and need to be dealt with first. Again, this is a great thing to do first thing as priorities may have changed since the day before, and you may need to rearrange the jobs you'd planned to do.

- If working, set time to meet regularly with your line manager and/or team. This is essential for managing your time as you may be able to avoid wasting precious minutes or hours you've set aside for something that's either not really needed or that could be delegated to others. Actually, it's important to do this at home too - we often find a lack of communication between those we are close to, as we half expect our loved ones and close friends to know things automatically...

Daily and Weekly Reviews

Let's look more closely at how to plan regular reviews to keep on top of your tasks and appointments.

Your tasks are the jobs you need to do, or have been asked by others to do, and will take varying amounts of time. You will have used the Time Matrix to prioritise and put these jobs into some sort of order, and will be placing them in your calendar. But then what? Is that it? Well, no, we can't just leave it at that, with the jobs sitting there waiting until the allotted time to action what's required. As we've already discussed, other more important or urgent jobs come along and steal our time from us. So, we need to review the calendar and bookings regularly.

How often is 'regularly'? Well, it's important to review your calendar on both a daily and weekly basis.

The Weekly Review

Your weekly review should be to look back over your last week as well as the next 7 days. Why the past week? Well, even though the time has gone and it can't be changed, you can still learn valuable lessons from looking back at the jobs and appointments that you *had* planned to do. Did you do them as you'd hoped? Did they get rescheduled, and if so, why? Think about unexpected chores or jobs that came in and that you hadn't planned for. What about if you block out some time next week to make sure you can deal with these eventualities should they arise?

And, how did your prioritisation work out? Was it accurate or did you think something was more important and urgent than it turned out to be? And, how did it feel doing some of those jobs at those particular times? Did you find you struggled to concentrate after 3pm in the afternoon? If so, next week move those jobs to earlier in the morning and put something a little more physical towards the end of the day.

A weekly review is good to do on a Friday afternoon, but it can be done at any time during the week, whatever works for you. I personally like a Friday afternoon as it means I start fresh on a Monday morning. But, for those that are shift-workers for example, a totally different day (or night!) might be better.

The Daily Review

As well as a weekly review, you should be aiming for a daily review too. Spend time each morning (or a more suitable time) to manage your list of appointments and chores so that you can look at the day ahead and make any necessary adjustments. An important job that you put in your calendar yesterday may now not be quite as important, or could have been pushed down the list by a more pressing task. Be realistic about what you can achieve and say no where necessary. This may mean declining meetings that you don't need to attend, deleting tasks that are not necessary and sending messages to let people know you are working on a response which, although won't be done today, now has a more realistic time for achievement.

So, you've reviewed your tasks and jobs - let's now look at how to book appointments into your Microsoft® Outlook calendar. It's up to you how much detail you put in, but the software offers far more than a simple scheduling of an appointment.

Adding Appointments

The Microsoft® Outlook calendar can be used to schedule appointments, organise meetings and events and to plan your To Do list. The more you use it, the more control you'll have over your day (or night if you're a shift worker!) And, if sharing your calendar in the workplace, Microsoft® Outlook offers the added benefit in that your colleagues will be able to see that you're busy and this will further help you to protect your valuable time.

You can view the Calendar in different ways, depending on the level of detail you want to see. Click on the Calendar icon in the navigation bar

and then use the Home ribbon to change the view.

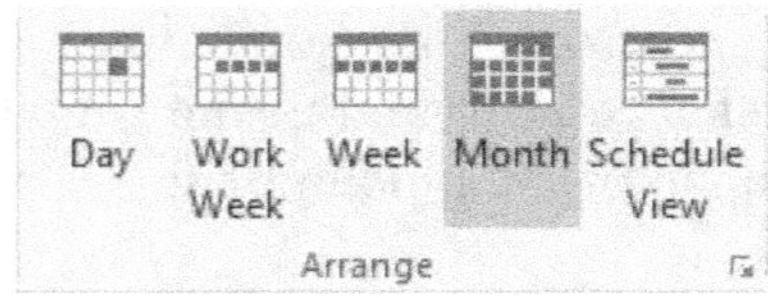

The views available are:
* Day
* Next 7 Days
* Work Week (Monday to Friday with weekends omitted)
* Week (a full 7-day week)
* Month

Clicking the Today icon will take you straight to 'Today' if you're not already there, rather than you having to scroll around the dates to navigate.

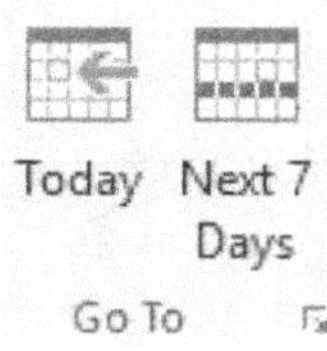

The appointment feature can be used to enter anything which requires you to allocate some time for a particular job or task. This could be for a job you need to complete, such as going through paperwork or working on a project. Or, it could be for a meeting between you and at least one other person. Meetings are covered in a later chapter.

To add an appointment:

*   Select the required date
*   Click the New Appointment icon on the Home Ribbon

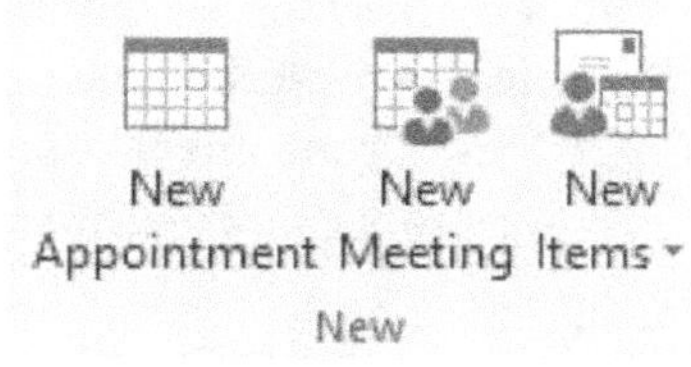

*   In the appointment window, type a subject and location (note: the location is not mandatory but can be helpful)

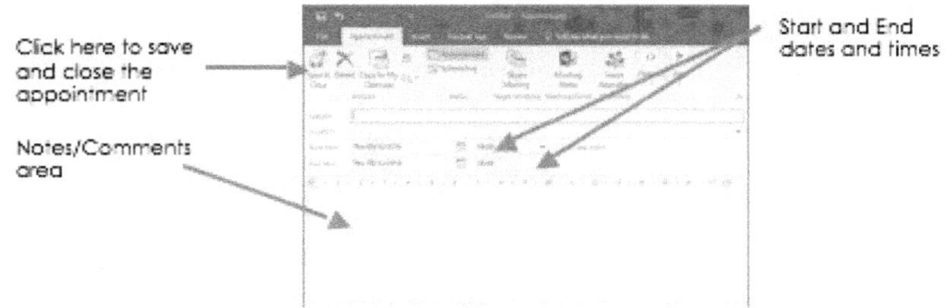

*   Select the Start and End time
*   Type any additional comments in the big white area of the window. This could be information you need, reference numbers, phone numbers etc.

- Click Save and Close

There are other features you can use when creating an appointment. For example, you can set a reminder – this can notify you in advance of an appointment so you don't accidentally forget about it. Although it only offers up to 2 weeks prior to the appointment, you can enter anytime you want by just typing it in the field.

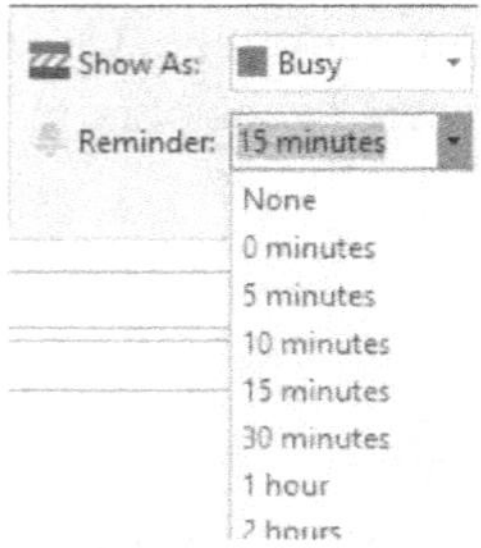

It may be that your appointment is an all-day event – this is for something that is not time restricted, such as an anniversary or birthday. Just tick the All Day Event check box in the appointment window.

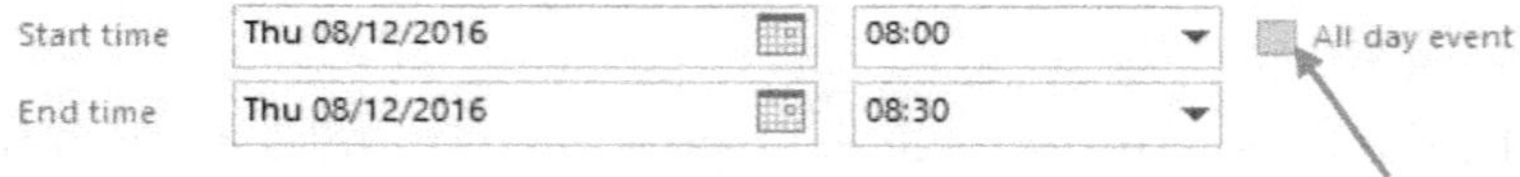

You can mark the appointment time as either free, working elsewhere, tentative, busy or out of office. A different coloured bar will be displayed beside the appointment making it easier to spot on your calendar.

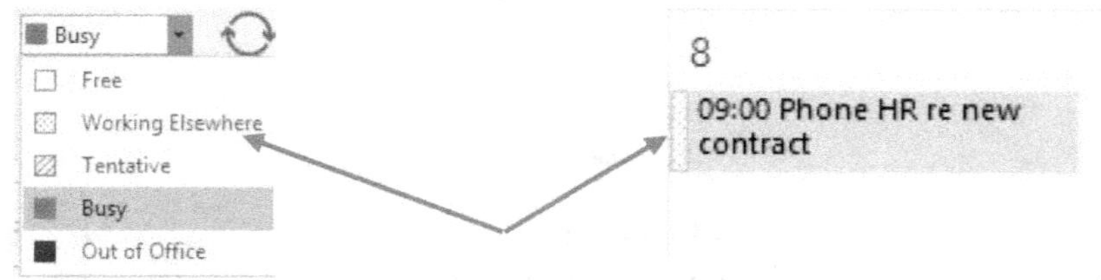

Selecting Private will mean that although your calendar may be viewed by others, they would not be able to see the details of the appointment – it will just show as 'busy'. However, you will still be able to see the full details in your own calendar with a small padlock symbol alongside to indicate the privacy setting.

Appointments can also be created by double clicking the calendar, or by clicking once on the Calendar and typing. If using the click and type method, you won't be presented with the appointment window but it's a great way to quickly schedule something in. You can always add to it later.

The calendar is only truly useful if you keep it up to date so let's have a look at that next.

Changing Appointments

So, you've started to use your calendar which means you are actively protecting your valuable time but it's important to remember that it has to be kept up to date and accurate if it's to function well. If you don't do this, you might find yourself forgetting appointments, getting booked up by others when you're busy and having your time well and truly stolen. Besides, if you don't know what you're doing each day, how is anyone else expected to? Investing the time in maintaining that calendar is well worth it and, if you make it part of your daily routine, it will soon be done on auto-pilot without you having to even think about it.

So, how do you change appointments? Well, one way is to simply click and drag to move it from one date/time to another. This is great if it's only moving a little bit of distance but not as easy if, for example, you're moving it to the next month. So, you can double click the appointment to reopen its window and then amend it from there. Just remember to click save and close.

If you want to extend or reduce the time of the appointment, there's no need to go into the Appointment window – just make sure you're in Day view and then click and drag the top or bottom edge of the appointment.

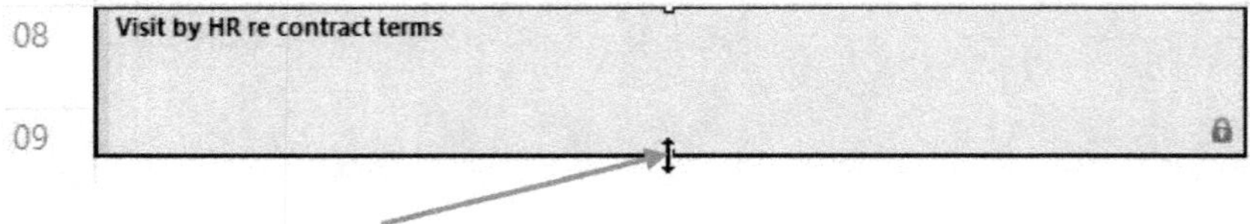

And, it may be that the appointment is no longer needed. So, whilst viewing the calendar (rather than being in the Appointment window), select the appointment and click the Delete icon on the Appointment ribbon. Pressing the Delete key on the keyboard works too.

So, appointments are pretty easy to modify meaning there's no excuses for letting the calendar get out of date. Just do it as soon as you know it needs changing or else there's a risk you might forget. Remember that you can adjust the times and dates, add extra information and also delete, all in the matter of seconds.

What about appointments that might be regular, such as a weekly task to check on a project, or to ring a family member or friend? These are known as recurring appointments. Let's see them in action!

Scheduling Recurring Appointments

You may find that some of your appointments occur on a regular basis and you don't want to be spending lots of time entering each appointment one at a time – remember, this book is all about managing your time better! So, let's take a look at how to schedule a recurring appointment.

When you create a new appointment you'll see a Recurrence icon in the Ribbon.

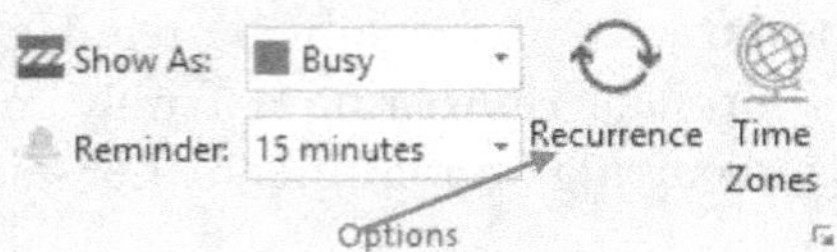

Clicking this icon will take you into the Recurrence window.

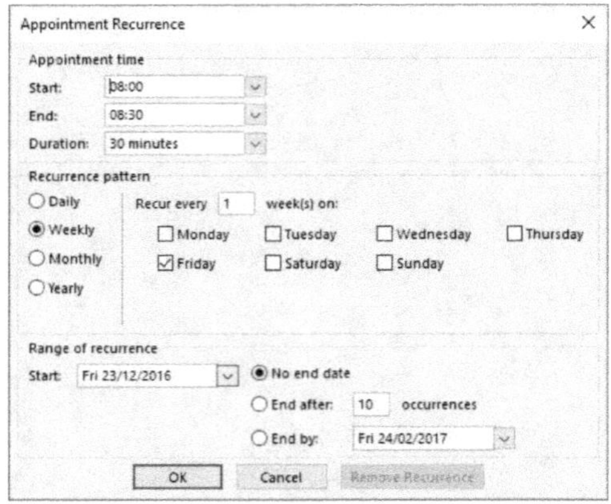

You can enter the start, end and duration of the appointment and then choose a recurrence pattern. The pattern will vary depending on whether it is the daily, weekly, monthly or yearly option that has been selected.

Once everything has been set it is time to choose the range of recurrence – when will the recurrence end? This can be a date, after a set number of times or no end date at all. And that's it!

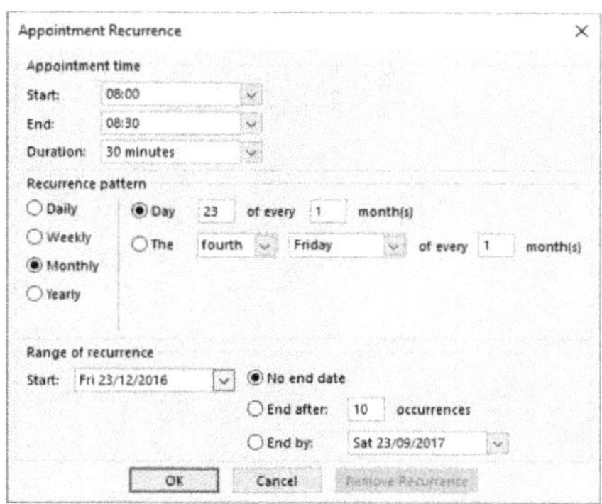

You'll recognise a recurring appointment in your calendar as you'll see a small circular arrow next to it.

When you modify a recurring appointment, or delete it, a window will appear which asks if it is only the one occurrence you wish to change, or all future events too.

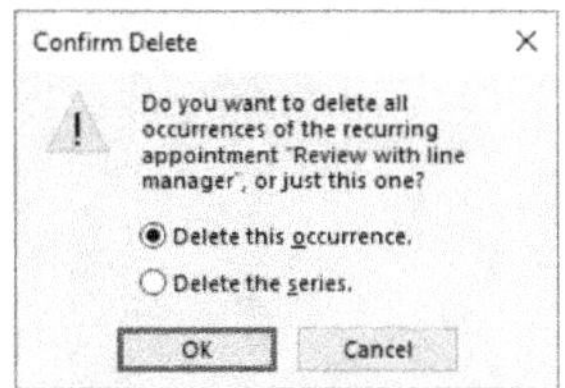

So, we've seen how we can create appointments just for ourselves. But, what about when we want others involved? In the next section we'll be looking at meetings and how best to arrange them.

Meetings

Scheduling a Meeting

Scheduling a meeting is very similar to creating an appointment. The only difference is that we invite others to attend.

You can either:

- Create a new appointment as before, and then invite attendees
Or
- Click the New Meeting icon on the Home tab of the ribbon

- If you choose to create a normal appointment, you'll see the Invite Attendees icon on the Appointment Ribbon.

- When you click it, it will take you to the same screen as if you had clicked the New Meeting icon.

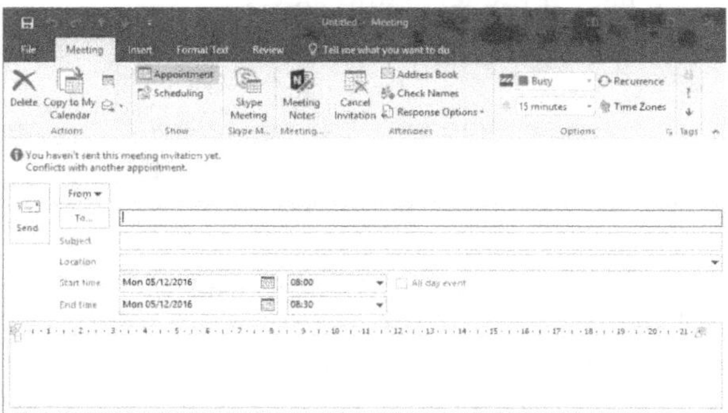

- Enter the Subject, Location, date and times. The subject should make it very clear what the meeting is about and will help to ensure that the relevant people attend. The Location is not a mandatory field but is very helpful as it tells the attendees where to meet.

- You'll see the 'To' field at the top of the window, similar to what you see if creating a new email message.

- Choose the people you want to invite to the meeting by entering their names in the To field, or by clicking the To button which allows you to insert the names into the Required, Optional or Resources fields.

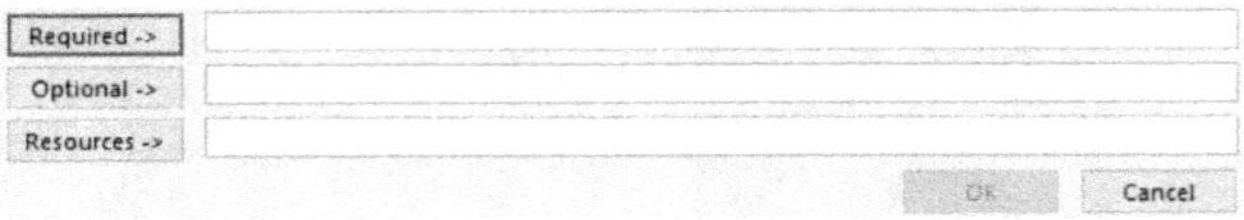

If using Microsoft® Outlook at work, you can really benefit from the fact that Calendars are shared across the organisation when trying to arrange a meeting. To see who is free to attend once you've entered names into the recipient fields, click the Scheduling icon.

Anyone that has been invited, including you as the organiser, will be displayed in a list on the left hand side.

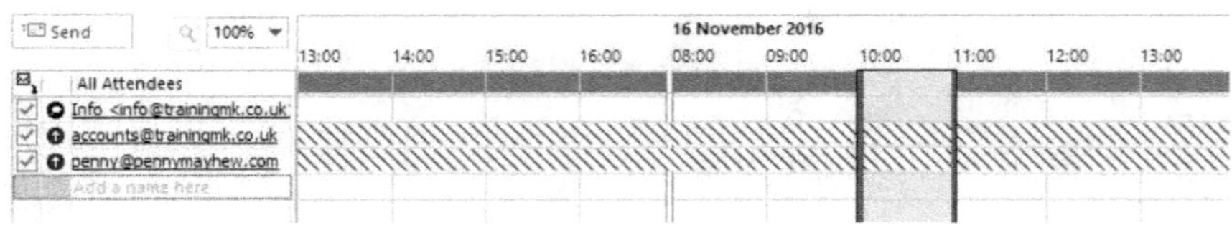

The availability of each person will show on the right in the form of coloured lines: Blue (if busy), purple (out of office) or stripy (tentative). You may also see another stripy kind of line which means that there's no information available. This is usually when you don't have access to their calendar or to the network.

If you need to adjust the time of the meeting you can click and drag the vertical slider to an alternative position. It might not always be possible to find a time that everyone can make, but at least you'll be able to go with the majority.

Once ready, click the Send button and your invite will be on the way!

An important point to consider is when it's appropriate to call a meeting. A meeting is very appropriate when:
- More than 10 long messages have gone back and forth amongst several people
- A new group of people are working together for the first time
- Collaboration is needed
- When it's the most efficient way to move forward

And, once you've decided that the meeting is necessary, next you need to make sure that the right people are attending. You should only invite the attendees that really need to be involved. Remember, the more people that attend, the more difficult it is to control the meeting and to reach key decisions. But, at the same time, if a decision needs to be made, you have to have the right people there - the decision makers. Without them, the meeting is generally a waste of time and resources. It's a fine balance between the two and you must get it right to avoid wasting a lot of time and energy. We've all been at meetings where we've sat there wondering *why...* Or when it's been hijacked by attendees that are really not even supposed to be there.

So, you've sent out the invites and now it's time to wait for the RSVPs to come flying in. It's a bit like organising a party! In the next chapter we'll look at how you can track the responses so that you know who is coming along, who has declined and who hasn't replied.

Tracking Responses

There's nothing worse than turning up as the organiser of a meeting and having no idea about who may, or may not, join you. Here's where your personal assistant steps in by tracking the meeting responses.

To track the responses:

- Find your meeting in the calendar and click to select
- On the Meeting Ribbon click the Tracking icon

All of the invited attendees will be listed with their responses.

Name	Attendance	Response
Info <info@trainingmk.co.uk>	Meeting Organizer	None
penny@pennymayhew.com	Required Attendee	Accepted
accounts@trainingmk.co.uk	Required Attendee	Declined
Add a name here		

You'll be able to see who is coming, who has declined and who hasn't answered yet, giving you the opportunity to chase those attendees before the meeting takes place.

The list of responses will also help you check that the decision makers will be present. If they're shown as having declined the invite, then it may be best to reschedule the meeting. If you don't, there's a very high chance that you'll need to postpone it part way through and organise it for an alternative time which will definitely not be good for your Time Management!

Cancelling and Rescheduling

Your meeting is arranged, you're feeling super-organised and on top of everything, but then it all falls apart... the room isn't available, you have other demands that take priority, some of the attendees are suddenly tasked with a more important matter... What do you do? Well, remember how important it is to keep your calendar up to date. It's time to amend or delete that meeting.

Meetings can be easily cancelled, but it's only the original organiser (i.e. the person that sent out the invites) that can do so. If it wasn't you that arranged it, get hold of the person that did and ask them to cancel asap so everyone is aware.

To cancel the meeting:

* Open the meeting in the calendar
* Click the Cancel meeting icon on the Meeting Ribbon

* Type a message in the email so that you can tell people why it is being cancelled
* When you click Send, all attendees will receive a cancelled meeting notification. You won't have to send an email to each attendee one at a time, it will be all be done for you with just a few clicks.

When the recipient opens the notification it will provide them with the option to remove the appointment from their calendar. This means they won't have to do it themselves and ensures their own calendar is kept up to date.

Instead of cancelling the meeting you may choose to reschedule it instead. Maybe the room is only available half an hour later, or the bulk of attendees can't make it until a later date. Existing meetings can be rescheduled easily, automatically sending out an updated meeting request to all attendees. How great is that? It's that Personal Assistant working hard again for you!

To reschedule a meeting (note: it can only be rescheduled by the original creator of the meeting):

* Open the meeting in the calendar

* Select a new date/time
* Click the scheduling icon to check attendees' availability
* Click back on the appointment tab
* Click the Send Update icon

The meeting will be automatically moved to the new date and time in the organiser's calendar and for any of the attendees that accepted the update.

So, we've seen how easy it is to either cancel or reschedule a meeting meaning there's no excuses for not keeping your own calendar up to date. We're now ready to move on to Tasks. It's time to start working on that To Do list...

What's On Your To Do List?

Making a List of Things to Do

We are all multi-tasking today more than ever before. It's now almost an expected way of life, juggling jobs to do and multiple responsibilities, all at a quick pace. It's inevitable that we'll forget something important at some stage, whether it's someone's birthday, an insurance renewal or a project deadline.

Keeping a To Do list really helps to keep on top of things. In fact, it's the only way if you want to ensure you do not forget something. It helps you to keep a record of everything you need to do and to prioritise your list in terms of urgency and importance. You'll feel more focused and better prepared, safe in the knowledge that you haven't forgotten anything important, and able to focus your time and energy on high value activities.

Keeping tasks in your head does not work... and keeping a paper list doesn't particularly function well either. Paper lists cannot be kept up to date easily or rearranged, and they can be lost or misplaced. Ever found a post it note, full of things to do in tiny writing, stuck to your shoe or at the bottom of a briefcase?

Now, before you have a go at creating the list, it's important to establish the difference between a task and a calendar appointment. Actually, for some people, they may choose to put everything into the Calendar and not work with a Task list at all. This can work, but may be time consuming.

The To Do list is really designed more for those things that are not time-bound in terms of the duration needed to do them. So, putting them in the calendar would be difficult as it's not an accurate way of blocking out time to allocate to the Task. For example, buying a card for someone or renewing your car insurance may not need to be done at a specific time or even date, but they are still important things to do which will have consequences if forgotten. A To Do list would be perfect.

Have a go now, on paper, at listing the tasks that you currently need to complete. These are all the things on your mind, as well as on lists you may already have completed (including those from earlier chapters in this book). Think of everything: cards to buy and post, things you need to get, renewals due, letters to send, ongoing projects that need attention etc. If they're large tasks, break them down into small bite-sized chunks. It can be overwhelming to plan big tasks as you know how time consuming it will be and, if you haven't the time right now to complete it, you will put it off. But in small chunks you can chip away at those jobs and see them diminish.

Next, get that list and start to prioritise the items listed. Use the Time Matrix to help you. Write a number next to each one to put them in order; for example, use 1 as most urgent and 5 as not really urgent at all. Finally, write next to each how much time you think you need to allocate in order to complete it.

If a task is going to take a long time, or is 'time bound', (i.e. needs to be done by a set date or time) then consider moving it into the calendar rather than creating it as a task. Make a note next to it to show it needs an appointment - in fact, you know how to do it now, so you can go straight to the Calendar and enter it there.

For the rest, we'll enter them as a Microsoft® Outlook task. Before we see how, it's worth thinking about how to record the tasks you need to do which pop into your head at the times when you don't have paper and pen, or Microsoft® Outlook, available. For example, those that you find yourself thinking about whilst driving or when you're at home and can't find the one and only pen that seems to exist in the house (and that others pinch!) ... If this happens, then consider using a voice memo function on your mobile phone or other device. They're great and will allow you to record the task in Microsoft® Outlook when back in the office or home.

So, you've got your list of tasks, let's now get them into Microsoft® Outlook!

Ticking Off the List

You've made your To Do list, you've worked out when things need to be done by and which are the most important, so now it's time to get them into Microsoft® Outlook so you can really benefit from the tools it provides to help keep that Task List in check. Now, there's a couple of ways you can enter tasks, so let's take a look at each one.

Remember that To Do pane on the right hand side of the screen when viewing your emails? The area that sits underneath the calendar and appointments shows any tasks outstanding, as long as you have chosen to display this option.

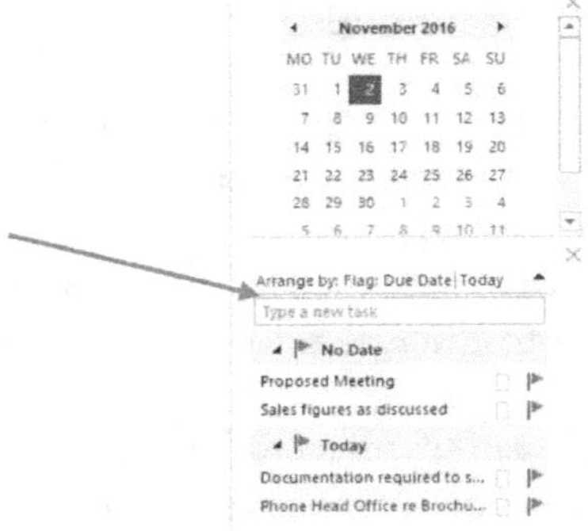

It also lets you add new tasks very quickly. Just type into the field and press enter, it's as simple as that. Maybe it's a reminder to ring someone, or collect something on the way home. Or perhaps it's to do with a project. Just make sure that the text you enter makes sense so you understand it. You don't want to be wasting valuable minutes trying to decipher a random phrase.

Once a task is complete you can click the flag and it's removed from the list. And there's no better feeling than ticking off those jobs to do!

If you want to micro manage your tasks, or add further details, then go to the Tasks area of Outlook (via the Navigation pane).

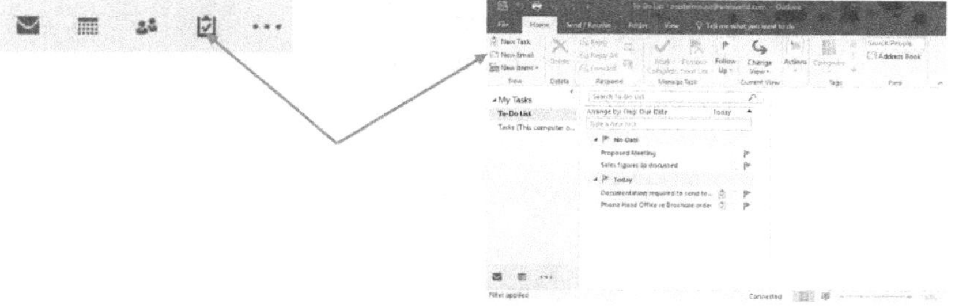

- Click the New task icon on the Ribbon

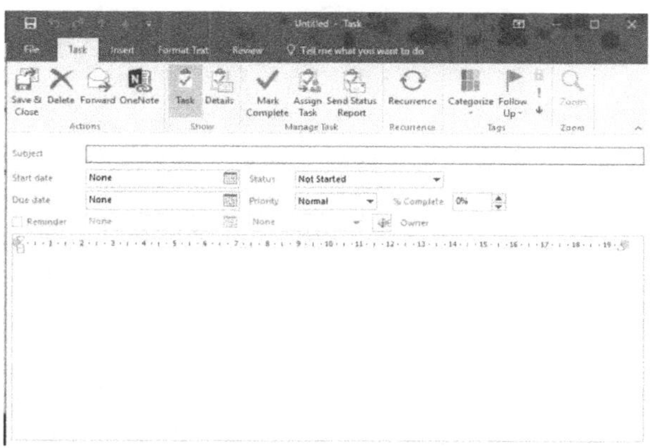

- Enter a subject for the task
- Set a start and due date (this is great for project planning, where you may not want to start the task straight away)
- Change the status if required to show if the task has not yet started, is in progress or has been completed. This helps you to keep track of what you've got going on at any one time
- If you wish, you can choose the priority. Again, it's great for when you're restricted in time and might want to work on the most urgent/high priority tasks first
- Select a % complete if you wish. This is when it can become quite time consuming, as you'd need to keep this regularly updated if it's going to be of benefit to you. So, you need to weigh up the advantages and disadvantages of using this field
- Set a reminder if required
- The comments box can be used to include further details of the task. This can help to keep everything in one place, so you're not having to search around for documents or text that you need.

There's more information you can enter too, try clicking on the Details icon and you'll see you can enter further information such as Contacts and Mileage etc.

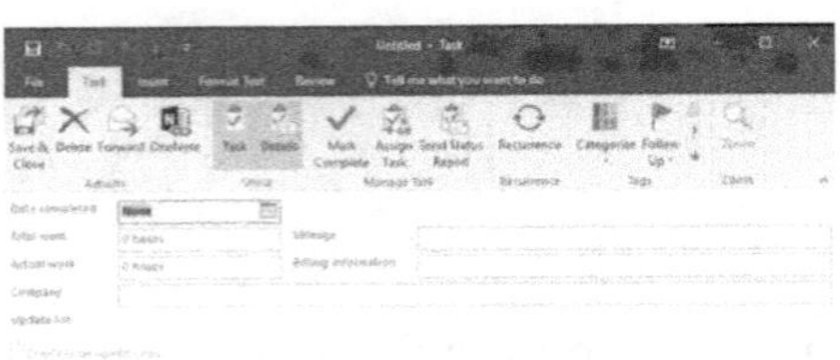

- When ready, click Save and Close

You can return to the task at any time by double clicking it – this will open up the Task window allowing you to make any modifications required.

Marking tasks as complete is easy when in the Task area of Microsoft® Outlook. Just click the Mark Complete icon on the Home Ribbon or click the check box next to the task

Completed tasks are shown with a line drawn through. This helps you keep a record of the work you've done, and is also a check point if you're unsure where you've got up to, or what still needs to be completed.

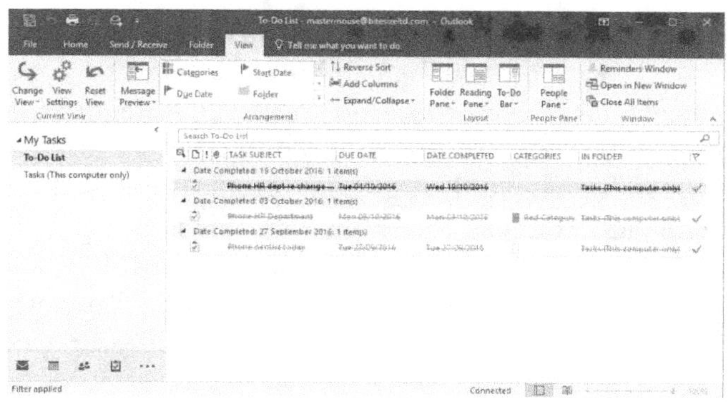

Remember that tasks can be as brief or as detailed as needed and that they allow you to keep everything in one place. Is there anything else you can do with Tasks to help stay even more organised? Well yes, let's see how we can group tasks together. We're going to examine Categories.

Working with Categories

Let's get our tasks even more organised! A Category is a colour code and keyword that helps to keep track of different items. Although we're looking at Tasks, Categories can be used for emails, appointments and contacts too. However, this is not possible when using particular types of email account, such as an IMAP, and so it is not covered in the book. But, after learning how to Categorise Tasks, you can apply the same techniques to emails etc if your account lets you.

Categories work particularly well with Tasks. You can easily find, sort, filter or group categorised items. So, for example, a colour category could be applied to Tasks relating to a particular meeting, phone calls you need to make or a holiday that you've booked.

In terms of time management, these are some recommended categories which could help you work more efficiently with your Tasks:

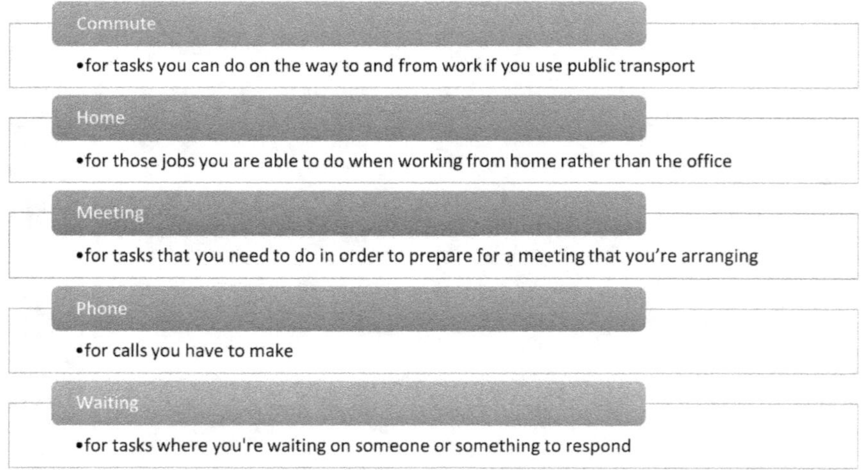

Categories really are a great time management tool. Now we know what Categories are, let's explore how to assign and modify them.

Assigning Categories

There's plenty of colours to choose from when it comes to Categories. 25 in fact! To start to work with Categories and assign them to tasks, first of all open the Task you want to categorise. Then, click the Categorize icon on the Task ribbon.

- Click All Categories to take you to the Colour Categories window.

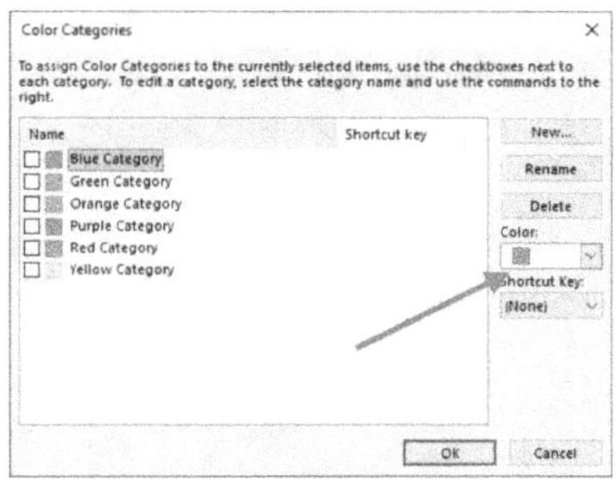

When you first use Categories you'll see that they are listed as Red Category, Blue Category etc. But, these can be amended to make them a little more user friendly. Before assigning a Category, select it and choose Rename. Name it something more appropriate, such as Holiday Planning or Project Meeting, for example. You can change the colour too by clicking the Colour drop down arrow.

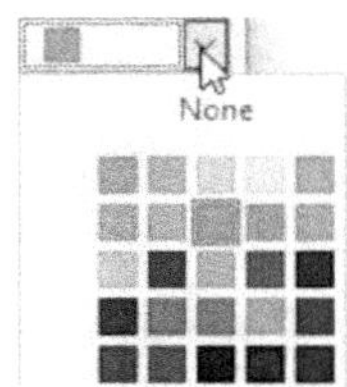

- You can apply further Categories if required. Once finished, click OK. The Task will now show the Colour Category and name within the Task Window.

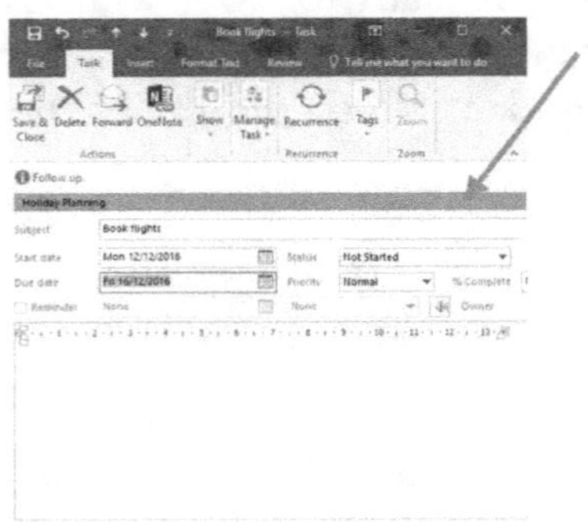

- Once finished, click to Save and Close. You will see the colour Category appear in the list of Tasks.

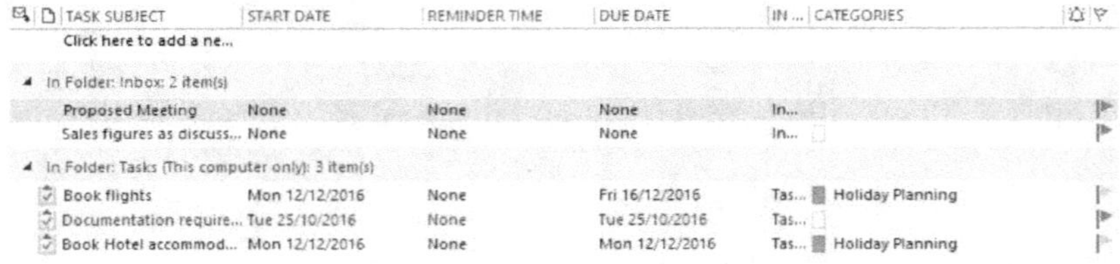

It's not a bad idea to get your Categories set up in one go, ready to apply. Use the New button to add further Categories to the list, should you need to.

Categories are easily removed by opening the task, clicking the Categorize icon and selecting Clear All Categories. Or, go to Categories and remove the tick from the Categories no longer needed for that task.

Once you've categorised your tasks you can sort them so that related tasks are grouped together. When in the Task list view, click the Categories heading and the tasks underneath will be sorted by the Category groups. A great Time Management technique, as it saves you from scrolling around and trying to find items, risking omitting something important. Imagine categorising tasks with the name of a meeting they're related to – if you sort it into order it virtually creates an agenda. Give it a go!

Do you remember the chapter about delegation? Well, we're going to return to the subject next. You've a list of tasks to work through but it doesn't necessarily mean it's you that has to do them all. What if there's someone else that can help so that you can get on with your other jobs? Let's talk delegation!

Delegate!

We've already looked a little at delegation and it really is one of the most important Time Management skills to get to grips with. It's not just a case of it benefiting *you* - delegation will enable you to develop and motivate those working *with* you, both at home and in the work place. They will gain experience of new activities and take on higher responsibilities. But, delegation has to be handled correctly.

When looking through your task list and deciding whether to delegate to others, always follow the rules:

* Is the task suitable to be delegated?
* Why are you delegating this task? What are you, and the person to whom it is being delegated, going to get out of it?
* Is the person you are delegating the task to capable of completing the job? Do they understand what needs to be done?
* Be specific about what you want to be achieved, and how you will measure the success.
* Agree a deadline - when does the task need to be finished?

In Microsoft® Outlook, tasks can be assigned to any person listed in the global/personal address lists and the task will be sent to that recipient by email.

* Create the task as normal OR, if already created, double click the task to open it.
* Click the Assign Task icon on the Task ribbon

* In the To field, enter the address name of the person it is being assigned to
* Click the Send button

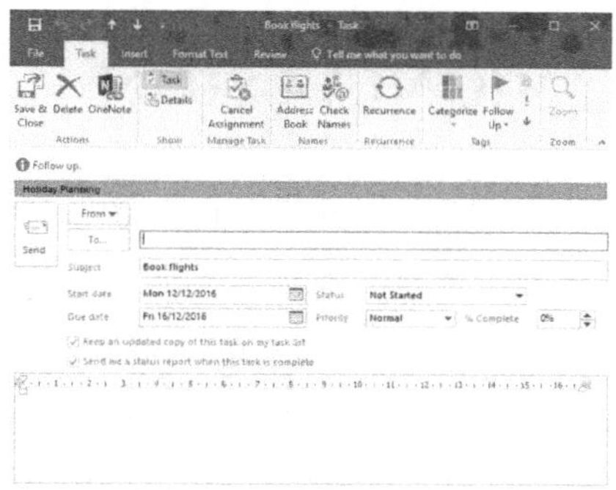

The assignee will receive a Task Request email which allows them to Accept or Decline the Task. By default, an updated copy of the Task will be kept in the original owner's Task list. The original owner of the task will receive a notification of the Assignee's response (i.e. whether they accepted or rejected the Task) and is also sent a status report once the Task has been marked as complete. The assignee will see the Task go into their own Task list if they accept it. Rejecting will send it straight back to the owner.

So much easier than typing a long email to someone to ask them if they can do x, y and z for you, and then having to chase it up later only to find it's been forgotten. Remember that you still need to handle the actual delegation process and to make sure the assignee you're delegating to is the correct, and most appropriate, person for the job. Then, sit back and let Microsoft® Outlook handle it all for you.

CONCLUSION

We've looked at Time Management techniques and how to use Microsoft® Outlook to help apply them to your daily, busy life. You did it! Congratulations, you've completed the Time Management with Microsoft® Outlook book and it's been great having you with me. So, now it's time to put everything into practice and really start getting your Time Management skills fine-tuned. Remember, Microsoft® Outlook is just a tool, a handy piece of software that can help you keep organised. But, it's the mind-set that's more important, the way you think about your time and how you protect it. Unless you put these changes in place, Microsoft® Outlook will be of little use to you.

What do you think has been the most important skill you've learned, or that you feel will change how you manage your time the most? During this book you:

- identified your current Time Management strategies and found out where all that time goes. Was this a surprise to you? Did you realise how your time is allocated to different activities, and to other people (whether voluntarily or not)?
- explored various Time Management techniques that can be used in everyday life, whether at home or at work. Which one did you feel was most useful to you?
- saw how to take control of your emails and that Inbox which was fit to burst
- covered how an appropriate, efficient and effective folder structure within Microsoft® Outlook can help you better manage those emails
- looked at how the calendar can help protect your precious time. It's not just for appointments and meetings and it's essential to keep it up to date if it's really going to work
- identified how To Do lists (Tasks) can help you plan, prioritise and, hopefully, delegate some of those jobs you have to do

So, now you need to put one item right at the top of your To Do list, and that item is:

'Apply these new skills to my everyday life, kick out those time thieves and claim back my precious 'Me' time!'

Good luck, and remember that you can review the chapters at any time. And there's an online course available through my website too. **Just go to** www.pennymayhew.com **to find all the links you need.**

Thank you!

RESOURCES

For templates and other resources relating to the book please go to www.pennymayhew.com to download for free!

Links:

For help with Microsoft® Outlook (and other Microsoft® applications) go to https://support.office.com/en-gb/outlook

To learn more about the Pomodoro Technique (a great tool to help Time Management) go to http://cirillocompany.de/pages/pomodoro-technique/

http://www.businessballs.com/timemanagement.htm - Businessballs is a great website, with a wide range of tools, techniques, resources, advice, training etc on a bundle of topics, including Time Management

Apps and Software

http://antisocial.80pct.com - Anti-Social, an app to help you block any online distractions such as websites and social media, whilst you're working.

https://www.office.com to purchase Microsoft® Outlook and other Microsoft products ®

http://selfcontrolapp.com - a free Mac app to help void distracting websites (allows you to set blocks of time, and to add sites to a blacklist!)

Books and Further Reading:

There are many books out there about Time Management, but this is my absolute favourite. *'Thrive'*, by Arianna Huffington. http://amzn.to/2g9C3qq

Also, *'Chimp Paradox'* by Prof Steve Peters examines Mind Management in general and has some great hints and tips. http://amzn.to/2fRqf9W

Both books are available in other formats as well as through Amazon.

ABOUT THE AUTHOR

Penny has worked as a Training Consultant, Facilitator and Coach for over 20 years, delivering classroom training, 1:1 support and e-learning design and development for many individuals and organisations. To find out more, locate details of online courses, or just to say hi, please visit www.pennymayhew.com or contact Penny at penny@pennymayhew.com

In addition to non-fiction material, Penny has also published novels in the name of Penny Canvin which have received 4.5 star reviews on Amazon (www.pennycanvin.com).